Franz Kafka

Jeremy Adler is Professor of German at King's College London. He studied German at Queen Mary College (University of London) and was a Lecturer in German at Westfield College before being awarded a Personal Chair. He is a sometime fellow of the Institute of Advanced Study, Berlin, and a sometime scholar of the Herzog August Bibliothek, Wolfenbüttel. He has written books on Goethe's *Elective Affinities* (1987), produced (with Ulrich Ernst) a catalogue of visual poetry, *Text als Figur* (third edition, 1990), and edited the collected works of August Stramm (1990). With Richard Fardon he edited Franz Baermann Steiner's *Selected Writings* (1999) and recently edited Steiner's collected poems (2000). His edition of Hölderlin's *Selected Poems and Fragments* appeared in Penguin Classics. He has published several volumes of poetry, including *The Wedding and Other Marriages* (1980), *At the Edge of the World* (1995) and *The Electric Alphabet* (third edition, 2001). Jeremy Adler is married and lives in London.

Franz

Jeremy Adler

Kafka

OVERLOOK PRESS
WOODSTOCK & NEW YORK

First published in the United States in 2002 by
The Overlook Press, Peter Mayer Publishers, Inc.
Woodstock & New York

WOODSTOCK:
One Overlook Drive
Woodstock, NY 12498
www.overlookpress.com
[For individual orders, bulk and special sales, contact our Woodstock office]

NEW YORK:
141 Wooster Street
New York, NY 10012

Published by arrangement with Penguin Books Ltd.

A CIP record for this book is available from the Library of Congress

Printed and bound in Great Britain by The Bath Press

9 8 7 6 5 4 3 2 1
ISBN 1-58567-267-X

Contents

Acknowledgements

The reason why posterity's judgement of an individual is more correct than that of his contemporaries has to do with the dead. You only develop your own character after death, when you are alone...

Kafka, *He*

This picture-essay is much indebted to the large body of writing that has grown up around Franz Kafka. Since his death, there has been a steady stream of biographies, commentaries, textual criticism, and interpretations, not to mention picture books. Anyone writing on Kafka cannot but feel a debt to his friend, Max Brod. Although Brod's views have been criticized, they have outlasted his critics'. Then there are the scholars who founded modern Kafka studies: his biographer, Klaus Wagenbach (1954; 1964; 1985); the commentator, Hartmut Binder, with his *Kafka Handbuch* (1979); and the doyen of Kafka editors Malcolm Pasley and his colleagues, whose critical edition (begun in 1982 and still in progress) is the starting point for all new work. For Kafka's official writings and his life in the office, I have relied on Klaus Hermsdorf's edition of the *Amtliche Schriften* (1984).There has been much recent research on Kafka's life, and I have profited from Rotraut Hackermüller's moving book on his last years (1990), Anthony Northey's delightful

Kafka's Relatives (1991), Alena Wagnerová's intriguing family history (1997), the invaluable *Kafka Chronik* by Roger Hermes *et al.* (1999), and Binder's fascinating book on Prague cafés (2000). The major critical studies by Wilhelm Emrich (1958), Walter Sokel (1964) and Heinz Politzer (second edn, 1966) provide a basis for modern readings, firmed up by Peter Beicken's critical introduction (1974). Since then, books like Ritchie Robertson's *Kafka: Judaism, Politics, and Literature* (1985), Mark Anderson's *Kafka's Clothes* (1992), and Scott Spector's *Prague Territories* (2000) have further contextualized Kafka's work. The references detail the German sources for some key quotations. My bibliography offers a selection of further reading in English.

Paul Keegan, formerly of Penguin Books, and Tony Whittome, of Random House, kindly presented me with several English Kafka translations. Kafka's style, so apparently simple, is subtle, nuanced and evocative, often allowing very different readings. In order to bring out the specific sense under discussion, I have translated directly from the originals, but have consulted the standard versions by the Muirs, Malcolm Pasley, and others, from whom I have gratefully adopted certain turns of phrase. As to the names of Prague streets, Bohemian villages, and so on, Kafka uses their German forms. It is difficult to be absolutely consistent in this matter. I have retained the German versions, except where there are standard English equivalents (such as Old Town Square). To enable the reader to negotiate modern Prague, I have added the current Czech names in parentheses. Regarding Kafka's friend Hugo Bergman (with one 'n'), I have adopted the form of his name that he used in later life.

Many people have assisted me. Caroline Pretty, at Penguin, first suggested this book, determined its shape, and was unfailing in her aid. I would also like to thank everyone at Penguin who made producing this book such an enjoyable experience. Reinhard Pabst offered advice, help, and pictures; Klaus Wagenbach put his archive at my disposal; Jan Kaplan made his unpublished prints available; Hartmut Binder supplied some rare photographs; Ladislav Čižinsky found a view of Špindlerův Mlýn; I am also much indebted to Pernilla Pearce, our picture researcher, for drawing the illustrations together. As to the text, several friends and colleagues have commented in detail on a draft. For suggestions and corrections I am grateful to Hans-Gerd Koch, joint editor of the great critical edition; Peter Staengle, joint editor of the new facsimile edition; my colleague, John White; and the Prague poet, Franz Wurm. Above all, I am indebted to my wife, Eva.

Over the years, I have been drawn to Kafka's life and work in various ways. Here, I would like to record my debt to two of Kafka's nieces, Věra Saudková and the late Marianne Steiner, who shared their memories with me. It is to Marianne Steiner's memory that this little book is dedicated.

Jeremy Adler
King's College London

Franz Kafka

Preface

I am alone as Franz Kafka...

To Gustav Janouch

Franz Kafka's name has become synonymous with modernity. The searing images in his writing encapsulate a modern Hell. A travelling salesman wakes up one morning to find himself transformed into a giant insect. A banker is arrested for an unknown crime, and vainly battles with an omnipresent, inscrutable Law. In a penal settlement, a torture machine inscribes justice upon a victim's body. And a man attempts to enter an unreachable castle. As W. H. Auden recognized, this singular portrayal of people entrapped in contemporary society turns the central figure in Kafka's works into an Everyman, while Kafka himself is a modern Dante, embarking on a journey through Hell and Purgatory towards a Heaven whose very existence remains in doubt.

Although as a writer he may be less dazzling than Proust, less innovative than Joyce, Kafka's vision is more stark, more painful, more obviously universal than that of his peers. His life alone cannot explain this difference. Some things can be attributed to his origins. Others to circumstance. Some to

Gruss aus Prag!

K. Bellmann: Panorama of Prague from Letná Hill, 1899. Kafka's home town, the ancient capital of the heart of Europe, is like a time warp, fusing medieval, renaissance, baroque and art nouveau features. Around 1900, the combination of economic growth, industrialization, political strife, and cultural innovation turned the city into a burgeoning microcosm of modernity

chance. But most to his personality. The character reflected in his books has lent his name an eerie, almost magical, aura, and has practically become a cipher for the man. Indeed, when he transformed his own identity into that of his fictional characters, by abbreviating his name to 'K.' in *The Trial* and *The Castle*, Kafka reinforced its hieroglyphic quality. In turn, the adjective 'kafkaesque' has gained an independent life, denoting nightmarish situations, an all-pervasive bureaucracy, looming totalitarianism, infinite hierarchies, and a deep existential *angst*. For a writer's name to be used to define the real world like this is almost unique.

What was it about Kafka that enabled him to depict modern life more tellingly than his contemporaries? The identity of his personality and his writing, and of his writing with a modern, impersonal world, lies at the heart of his work. As an artist, he grew increasingly clear about the symbiosis between self, world, and writing. He willed it, he trained it, he lived it, and eventually, perhaps, he died for it. In a letter of 14 August 1913 he observes: 'I have no literary interests, but am made of literature, I am nothing else and can be nothing else.' Against the traditional image of the writer and his world, Kafka asserts their identity. On the one hand, like the *fin-de-siècle* dandy caught by the camera in 1905–6, complete

with bowler, dog, and cabaret-artist cum part-time prostitute, his life becomes the work of art; whilst on the other, an obsessive realist like Flaubert, his personality is effaced as it merges with his fiction. This tension is

View of the Prague Castle (Hradschin/Hradčany). Dating back to around 870, the castle was much expanded in later years, receiving its final form in the eighteenth century, and now consists of a large complex, including St Vitus's Cathedral. It was the official residence of the Czech Princes from around 894 until 1918, when it became the residence of the President of the Republic. A powerful symbol of political and religious authority, its buildings are echoed in *The Trial* and *The Castle*

one of the many paradoxes in Kafka, and defines the whole trajectory of his life, in which he transformed himself from an aesthete into an ascetic. This latter is his final identity, whose emaciated, haunting gaze we witness in the last portrait, taken when he was dying of tuberculosis in 1923–4.

As a writer, his affinities first lay with the decadent *fin-de-siècle*, then veered towards the violence associated with Expressionism, and finally reached a mode closer to the unadorned starkness typified by German *New Sobriety*. But Kafka belonged to no school. He stands alone – 'alone as Franz Kafka', he

The Prague skyline, viewed from the road beneath Chotek Park (Chotkovy Sady), Kafka's favourite walk.

once said. His unique appeal, therefore, ultimately rests on the simplest paradox of all: all human beings are the same, but everyone is human in their own way. His genius lay in so focusing on inheritance, family, circumstances, and character that their singularity reflected a universal law.

In his notebooks, he pondered deeply about his relationship to his times, implicitly locating his work in the tradition that stems from Baudelaire's *Fleurs du mal* when he observed that he had adopted the 'negativity' of the age. Unlike so many of his great contemporaries who did battle with modern social values – one thinks of the Viennese prophets Sigmund Freud, Arnold Schönberg, Karl Kraus and Ludwig Wittgenstein – instead of fighting the era, Kafka absorbed it. Thus, 'to a certain extent' he believed that he had earned the right 'to represent' his

Old Town Square (Altstädterring/Staroměstské náměstí) with the Gothic Town Hall and its famous astronomical clock. The historic centre of Prague, dating back to the tenth century. From birth to final illness, Kafka's life revolved around this square, and it features in his work from the very beginning, in *Description of a Struggle*, to the end, in *Josephine the Singer*. On the right at the end, the renaissance Haus zur Minute (Minuta), built in 1610, where the Kafkas lived from 1889–96.

age. In fact, he transposed the struggle into his own being: 'In the battle between yourself and the world, take the part of the world.' He portrayed evil unflinchingly and, although he recognized its power, he never quite relinquished the hopeless quest for an ideal. This desperate engagement with evil helps to explain how the man and his monstrous century appear to have united, producing an *oeuvre* in which his readers could recognize Kafka's problems as their own. The stark simplicity with which he represents ordinary life – in the family, in a bank, in a village – is shaped by the relentlessness with which he seems to invoke absolutes in an insecure world. This, too, is modern. He recognizes humbly that his existence lacks any kind of basis, comprising no more than 'universal human weakness', and sees his job in the need to create his own 'ground' – a task, he concedes, which others have also attempted. However, in a phrase that corrects his humility, he questions whether anyone else attempted this task 'to the same extent'. Here speaks the artist as hero. The avant-gardist, advancing into uncharted territory. For Kafka, this is not just an intellectual or an aesthetic issue. It is more existential, more spiritual, yet conceived in surprisingly world-historical terms. In defining his identity, Kafka casts an eye to the east, but speaks as a western world citizen, using imagery that recalls Chagall: 'Unlike Kierkegaard I was not led into life by the hand of Christianity ... and unlike the Zionists, I did not catch hold of the last tassel of the Jewish prayer shawl as it flew away.' After the nineteenth century had sought to make art a religion, Kafka – renegotiating Kierkegaard's *Either/Or* – drew upon religion to make modern art. Concluding this reflection on his negative task with the typically archaic power his utterance can command, he revises God's words in Revelation I:viii, to replace prophetic certainty with his own, modern dilemma: 'I am an end or a beginning.'

Kafka aged about five. 'I would have needed a little encouragement, a little friendliness, a little openness towards my way ...' (*Letter to My Father*, 1919)

A Prague Childhood

I was brought up in the middle of town ...

Kafka, Diaries

Franz Kafka was born in his parents' home in Prague as the first child of Julie and Hermann Kafka on 3 July 1883. The house lay at the heart of Prague. In the centre of the Old Town, it adjoined Nicholas Church, and overlooked a small, nameless area at the edge of the breathtakingly beautiful Old Town Square. To the north and north-west, the Ghetto to which the Jews' dwellings had formerly been confined for centuries still stretched away towards the River Moldau (Vltava), which was traversed by Charles Bridge, lined with haunting statues. On the other side of the Moldau lies

Kafka's birthplace, the Baroque house No. 27/I, Zum Turm, at the corner of Karpfenstrasse and Enge Gasse (later Maislgasse) (Kaprova ulice / Maislova). Demolished in 1897–8, only the entrance survives. The area in front was recently named after Kafka, and the house now contains a small Kafka exhibit.

the Lesser Town (Kleinseite/Malá Strana), with its churches, palaces, and gardens steeply rising through winding streets to Hradschin (Hradčany), the area of the Prague Castle that dominates the town. For most of his life Kafka lived, worked, and wrote within a short walk of his birthplace. 'Do people think that I was brought up somewhere apart?' a story in his diary begins. 'No, I was brought up in the middle of town, in the middle ...' Prague provided the matrix

Clearance of the Prague Ghetto, begun in 1896: the area on which Niklasstrasse (Mikulášská, the modern Pařížská) was built, where the Kafkas moved in 1907.

Franz Kafka

of Kafka's experience, and – as Dublin provided the focal point for Joyce – the sites of his native city reappear in his works, at first realistically, as in *Description of a Struggle*, but later in shadowy, transmuted forms, as in *The Trial*, while its escutcheon features in *A City Coat-of-Arms*. Indeed, his young friend, the writer Johannes Urzidil, observed, 'Kafka was Prague, and Prague was Kafka.' But the ancient town with its medieval streets, its Gothic churches and baroque palaces was changing. The old Ghetto, to which – since 1849 – the Jews were no longer legally confined, had fallen into decay. Slums, brothels and crime peopled its narrow lanes. Modernization demanded clearance and reconstruction. Except for the monuments that survive today – the Jewish Cemetery, the Pinkas Synagogue, the Jewish Town Hall and the Old New Synagogue – the Ghetto was

Looking down towards the new bridge along Niklasstrasse (Mikulášská), which was created by the 'Haussmannization' of Prague. The Kafkas moved into number 36, the house at the far end on the right, in 1907.

demolished. As the Prague writer Oskar Wiener exclaimed in 1906, in characteristic *fin-de-siècle* voice: 'Prague, that unspeakably beautiful but dissolute Castle on the Vltava! Old Prague is dying, but a new, sober Prague is emerging from the massive stone among the rubble!' A long, straight road was driven through the labyrinthine Ghetto round the corner from Kafka's birthplace, leading past the Old New Synagogue to a new bridge across the river. The Kafkas moved into a newly built home here in 1907, an apartment at 36 Niklasstrasse (Mikulášská). Later, the road was renamed Paris Street (Pařížská). The modernizers had looked far to the west, and effectively

Kafka's father, Hermann Kafka (1852–1931). 'You are a real Kafka in strength, health, appetite, voice, rhetorical skill, self-satisfaction, superiority, stamina, quickness, insight, generosity, and of course you have all the errors and weaknesses that go with these qualities ...' (*Letter to My Father*, 1919).

imported the city which
Walter Benjamin called 'the
capital of the nineteenth
century' into their pictur-

Kafka's mother, Julie Kafka, née Löwy (1856–1934).
'... my mother was infinitely good to me ...'
(*Letter to My Father*, 1919).

esque town, turning Prague into what André Breton called
'the secret capital of Europe': a place where, politically, a new
century was forged, and all the arts flourished, including
architecture, painting, sculpture, design, music, theatre, and
literature. Prague history did much to inform Kafka's personality, and the clash between ancient and modern that issued
in this vibrant, modernist culture – rivalling that of Vienna
and Berlin – provided a central tension in his life.

The geographical position of Kafka's birthplace at the
Ghetto's edge mirrors the wider complexities, a pull between
east and west, found in his family, in Prague, and in Bohemia

Franz Kafka

Previous page The crossroads known as The Golden Cross (Goldenes Kreuz/Zlatý Kříž) at the lower end of Wenceslas Square (Wenzelsplatz/Vaclavské náměstí) leading into Am Graben (Na Příkopě) with the Powder Tower in the distance (*c.*1905). With its elegant shops, hotels and cafés frequented by writers and artists, the Graben was the major promenade for German-speaking Pragers, including Rilke, who cut a figure as a dandy here in the 1890s. It is often mentioned in Kafka's diaries.

itself. His origin was Jewish. His language was German. His town was predominantly Czech. His State and its educational system were Austrian. Yet there were convergences. As the writer Karel Čapek observed, even Bohemian Catholics were influenced by Jan Hus (whose monument stands in Old Town Square), and Jews like Kafka also shared the Hussite faith in the power of Truth.

Kafka internalized Prague's identities and divisions. Regarding his religion, he asked: 'What do I have in common with the Jews? I don't even have anything in common with myself.' As to language, he confessed that although German was his mother tongue, Czech lay closer to his heart. His physique proved similarly problematic. He complained that the 'bad clothes' he had to wear as a child damaged his 'posture', and even blamed his body for his own supposed 'failure': 'Nothing can be achieved with a body like this.'

His father Hermann was in reality, and even more in his son's perception, a large, strong man, whose personality typified the Kafka family's 'will for life, business, and conquest'. The family name (the Czech *kavka*) means 'jackdaw'. Hermann was born in 1852 in the almost wholly Czech village of Wossek (the modern Osek) in the district of Písek, Southern Bohemia. To heighten his own image as a self-made man he painted a picture of an impoverished childhood, but his father was, in fact, a well-respected and fairly prosperous butcher. Like so many Jews in the age of religious emancipation, which coincided with the era of industrial modernization, however, Hermann Kafka discarded his origins, gravitated to the 'liberal' city, and devoted himself to business. Having worked from the age of fourteen, and following military service, he settled in Prague in 1880. On 3 September 1882 he married Julie Löwy, and it was probably around this time that he founded his wholesale and retail business on the north side of Old Town Square, dealing in 'thread, cotton, and haberdashery' – wares that typified the new industries that had grown up in Bohemia, and the considerable wealth

Postcard with a view of Prague Castle, *c.*1908.

that they generated. In a memoir, Julie Kafka recalls her own, very different origins. She came from the spa town of Podiebrad (Poděbrady) on the Elbe (Labe), to the east of Prague. Her paternal grandfather, from the only branch of her family in which Kafka's diaries evince any interest, was a great scholar, noted for neglecting his business to devote himself to the Talmud. Kafka inherited the Löwys' gentler, more individualistic temperament, and he preferred the Löwys' company. He mediates this contradictory heritage in a brief tale, *A Cross-Breed*, with its 'peculiar animal', half-cat, half-lamb, which is perhaps only fit for another heirloom, 'the butcher's knife'.

The Prague which magnetized Hermann Kafka, like countless other countrymen, was in those days a thriving town, the capital of Bohemia, which itself was the fastest modernizing, most industrially advanced region in the Austro-Hungarian Empire. As a result of increasing urbanization, the Prague population doubled in the late nineteenth century and at the turn of the century it numbered 140,000, or around half a million including the suburbs. Czechs were in the majority.

Only 54,000 citizens classed themselves as German, half of these as Jews. The German speakers, the ruling class under the Habsburgs, had a strong presence, notably in the Old Town, evident in economic, social, political and cultural terms. There were several German newspapers, two German theatres, a German concert hall, and a German university. However, in the nineteenth century the renaissance of a Czech consciousness heralded a cultural and political rebirth, shaped by figures like Dobrovský, Jungmann and Palacký, who worked towards Czech political autonomy. The language was regenerated, and a new culture forged, epitomized by Smetana's *My Country* (1870), his opera *The Bartered Bride* (1866), and Božena Němcová's novel, *The Grandmother* (1855), one of Kafka's favourite books. Political unrest loomed large. Despite the fact that by 1883 (the year of Kafka's birth) the Czechs had the majority in the Bohemian Parliament, in 1893 the Viennese authorities imposed a state of emergency, and more troubles followed, until in 1913 Vienna revoked Prague's parliamentary powers.

Jews had lived in Bohemia for centuries. With the Enlightenment came emancipation, and as the Slavs sought autonomy, so did the Jews, who, having been granted permission to marry freely and, subsequently, to live outside the Ghetto, finally gained full citizenship in 1867. This entrenched another polarity within the Jewish community between the emancipated, westernizing modernizers centred in towns, and their orthodox brethren to the east, in Slovakia and Galicia. His later encounter with the eastern Jews was to prove pivotal in Kafka's birth as a writer. Zionism, inaugurated by Theodor Herzl's *The Jewish State* (1896), with its aspirations for a Jewish homeland, added a further, immensely productive dimension to Jewish national life, and also affected Kafka.

Such was the conflictual political, cultural, and national scene in Kafka's day. Indeed, the tensions between Germans

Previous page Zeltnergasse (Celetná), viewed from the Powder Tower. The main thoroughfare through the Old Town, leading from the Powder Tower to Old Town Square. The Kafkas lived at No.2 (Sixt Haus) from 1888–9, and at No.3 (Zu den drei Königen) from 1896–1907. Hermann Kafka's shop was at No.12 from 1906–12.

and Czechs were compounded by shared attitudes towards the Jews, with a new wave of anti-semitism during the 1880s which peaked in the so-called Hilsner affair of 1899, when – in medieval style – a Jew was accused of ritual murder. Kafka's *In the Penal Colony* confronts such barbarities with modern, liberal views. In politics, it was the liberals who gained the upper hand under the leadership of Thomas Garrigue Masaryk, himself the key 'Dreyfusard' in the Hilsner affair, who later orchestrated the declaration of independence after World War I. This contributed to the end of the Austro-Hungarian Empire, and gave rise to modern Czechoslovakia (made up of Bohemia, Moravia, and Slovakia), and the new geo-political configuration in modern Europe.

Although Kafka spent his childhood in Prague, it was not a peaceful life, the family being more preoccupied with the developing business than its offspring, except at mealtimes, so that the children were left to the servants. Kafka recalls that he 'lived alone for a very long time and had to struggle with nurses, child-carers, sarcastic cooks, and miserable governesses'. His birth was followed by that of two more boys, who both died in infancy: Georg, born in 1885, who died fifteen months later, and Heinrich, born in 1887, who died after six months. Three sisters survived into adult life: Gabriele, known as Elli, born in 1889, according to Kafka's *Letter to My Father* a 'slow, tired, fearful, bad-tempered, guilt-ridden, over-humiliated, wicked, lazy, miserly child'; Valerie, known as Valli, born in 1890, who Kafka claimed took after their kindly mother; and Ottilie, known as Ottla, born in 1892, 'a sort of Löwy endowed with the best Kafka weapons'. Early pictures

show the trio, dressed in identical clothes. His three sisters may sometimes be evoked in the strange symbolic triads that people his works, like the three identical lodgers in *The Metamorphosis*, who upset the Samsa family's already somewhat weird dynamics. The dead brothers may be echoed in the doubles associated with Kafka's heroes.

Kafka's sisters photographed around 1898. From the left: Valerie, known as Valli (1890–1942), Gabriele, known as Elli (1889–1942), and Ottilie, known as Ottla (1892–1943).

The family business, founded at 8 Old Town Square in 1882, moved to Stockhausgasse (Věžeňská) in 1885, then to 3 Zeltnergasse (Celetná) from 1886 until 1906, when Hermann gave up the retail shop and moved to number 12 where the wholesale business remained until 1912. It then transferred to the Kinský Palais at 16 Old Town Square until its sale in 1918. The theft of the family's laundry when Kafka was two and Hermann Kafka's occasional brushes with the law regarding his trade added to his worries. The growing family, notwithstanding a rising income and an improving position,

Old Town Square with the Thein Church (Týnský chrám). The Kinský Palais is on the left. Kafka's primary school was on the first floor. From 1912–18 Hermann Kafka's shop lay in the right wing (the name is just visible on the sign).

also entailed unrest, in that it occasioned frequent changes of address. In May 1885, the Kafkas moved to 56 Wenceslas Square (Wenzelsplatz/Václavské náměstí) for a few months, in September to house number V/187 in nearby Geistgasse (Dušní); then, in 1887, into 6 Niklasstrasse (Mikulášská), a year later to 2 Zeltnergasse (Celetná); and finally, in 1889, they were back at Old Town Square, where they lived for seven years in the medieval house known as *Minuta*, but then they moved again, this time to the first floor at 3 Zeltnergasse (Celetná), where Kafka, by now entering his fourth year at the Gymnasium, had a room to himself and, as a schoolfriend admiringly recalls, even his own desk. A peculiarity of this home was the interior window that looked directly into the Thein Church (Týnský chrám).

Kafka's mother records that he was 'a healthy but sensitive child', and the first photographs show a strong-willed, slightly quizzical, sometimes angry two-year-old. Aged four, he appears shy, hesitant, thoughtful; his eyes focused on the distance as if subdued, consumed by an infinite sadness.

Later in life, having encountered Freud's ideas, Kafka attributed his character and his writing to his childhood, and specifically to what he considered his father's malign influence. *Letter to My Father* paints him as a 'tyrant', exuding 'strength, noise, and anger', while his mother

Kafka aged about four. 'I was a frightened child, but in spite of that I was certainly difficult, too, as children are ...' (*Letter to My Father*, 1919).

appears as an affectionate woman, albeit wholly under her husband's domination. Kafka's earliest memories reflect this. One night, he recalls, he was being difficult. He begged for a drink of water which he may not actually have wanted, and his father responded by carrying him outside on to the covered balcony that overlooked the yard – the so-called *Pawlatsche* – 'and left me alone there in my shirt for a little while'. This caused 'inner damage'. One may compare the young Marcel in Proust's *À la recherche* ..., traumatized by his mother's failure to give him a goodnight kiss. In rehearsing his father's reaction, Kafka excludes the parental view: 'I could never connect what was for me a perfectly normal act, my pointless request for water, and the extraordinary terror of being carried outside.' If, as his *Letter to My Father* argues, Hermann Kafka was wilful, difficult, arbitrary, and obstinate, it would appear that the infant Kafka shared at least some of these qualities, which would have tragically provoked the conflict. Retrospectively, the trauma demonstrated to Kafka a gulf between crime and punishment, treated later in *The Trial*, and implies his early consciousness of an inner split. 'Years later, I still suffered from the tormenting idea that the huge man, my father, the ultimate judge, could come almost without any reason in the middle of the night, and carry me out of bed on to the *Pawlatsche*, and that for him I was such a mere nothing.' In another memory, Kafka recollects the shame he felt at his puny body when undressing beside his father at the swimming pool. But if his father embodied the nineteenth-century patriarch, the crass self-made man who, magnified in the child's eye, caused his little son excruciating pain, according to Kafka's schoolfriend, Hugo Bergman, as well as his niece Marianne – Valli's second daughter – Hermann Kafka was 'really quite ordinary'. Indeed, Kafka himself elsewhere evokes more sympathetic images. *Meditation* contains a piece, 'The Merchant', which seems to meld his father's worries with his own, solitary anxieties, whilst another, 'Clothes', betrays the delight in dress and fashion, evident throughout his work, that presumably originated in the ambience around his father's shop. Just as Kafka's allure owes much to his preserving a child-like freshness, it would seem that his earliest anxieties fed directly into his mature, painful depictions of humiliation, and his ruthless analysis of power.

The Artist as a Young Man

Here was my gymnasium, over there in the building looking across was my university, and a little further to the left my office. In this small circle – *and he drew a few circles with his finger* – my whole life is enclosed.

To Friedrich Thieberger

Kafka discovered his vocation in his schooldays. He attended the German primary school on the Meat Market (Fleischmarkt/ Masný trh) from 1889–93, where he excelled, being as a friend recalled 'a model pupil', and from 1893–1901 he went to the German Gymnasium in the Kinský Palais on Old Town Square. As a child he wrote playlets to perform with his sisters with titles like 'The Juggler', 'Speaking Photographs', and 'George of Podiebrad (Poděbrady)' – the

Kafka aged about thirteen

Kafka at the time of his matriculation in 1901.

legendary Czech hero from his mother's birthplace. At fourteen, as his classmate Hugo Bergman records, he decided to become a writer. His earliest surviving work, dated 20 November 1897, preserved in Bergman's common-place book, already bears Kafka's characteristic stamp:

There is a coming and a
    going,
A parting, and often – no
    meeting again.

Bergman stresses Kafka's early talent. One day, they passed a bookseller's in Old Town Square, and Kafka asked his friend to test his memory. To Bergman's amazement, Kafka could list every book and author in the window. One can only speculate about the boys' role in each other's development: the one a budding writer, the other a future thinker. Their later work, certainly, shows a remarkable convergence, in that Kafka's writings exhibit the same syncretism – the capacity to absorb contradictory sources – that Bergman advocated in religious matters.

Kafka's first plan for a novel, which he destroyed with all his other early writings, appears to have contained the seeds of his later work. It concerned a struggle between two brothers, 'one of whom went to America, while the other stayed behind in a European gaol'. Like other attempts to develop his own 'individuality', this work met with no encouragement: 'Family feeling gave me an insight into the cold space of the world that I had to heat with a fire which I first had to look for myself.'

The books he read outside school appear – as usual – to have made the greatest impact on Kafka. While at the Gymnasium, he discovered Heinrich von Kleist, whose plays and novellas demonstrate the chasm between earthly law and absolute justice. Years later, he still felt the 'fear of God' when reading Kleist's *Michael Kohlhaas* 'maybe for the tenth time', and recited it in public in the

Kafka's schoolfriend, Hugo Bergman (1883–1975). He served in the war and emigrated to Palestine in 1920, later becoming Vice Chancellor of the Hebrew University, Jerusalem. Although the young Kafka was critical of Zionism, in 1923, after hearing Bergman lecture, he contemplated emigrating to Palestine.

Jewish Town Hall. He even borrowed a central motif (Kohlhaas's horses) in *A Country Doctor*. Contemporary literature was also important for him. In 1899, the Bohemian-born social reformer Joseph Popper-Lynkeus published his *Fantasies of a Realist* which, being officially banned, proved particularly popular. These poetic miniatures provided a model for Kafka's *Meditation*. In the last piece, in which two friends hear the primal scream of Nature, one encounters the *angst* that became typical for the age, and was most memorably caught in Munch's *The Scream* (1893). Another early but abiding influence was Nietzsche, whose *Thus Spake Zarathustra* Kafka read in 1900. However, the passage which he chose for oral presentation in his final school year,

1900–1901, was the end of Goethe's artist tragedy, *Torquato Tasso*, one of the hardest, most frequently debated passages in German literature. Tasso's speech concludes with his credo:

And whereas Man in his
    anguish grows silent,
A god has taught me to say
    how much I suffer.

Judaism played no meaningful part in Kafka's upbringing. His *bar mitzvah*, for which he learned the Hebrew text by rote, took place on 13 June 1896, but he gained no insight into religion, and became an atheist. Bergman recalls their estrangement around 1899, when (outside school) Kafka sported the red carnation of the socialists, while he himself devoted himself to Zionism. Kafka's diaries record how as a schoolboy he engaged in 'Talmudic' debate with Bergman, refuting the thesis that God could be compared to a

Kafka at the time he entered university (1901).

watchmaker. In keeping with this early scepticism, influenced by his science teacher, Kafka read Darwin and Haeckel. An angry let-

The Pinkas Synagogue, founded in 1479 by Rabbi Pinkas, at the time of the clearance of the Ghetto. The Kafka family's place of worship. Today, the synagogue is a memorial to those killed in the *Shoah*.

ter from Bergman, written around 1902, offers a telling picture of his sardonic childhood friend. In outline, we recognize the adult: 'Since childhood you unconsciously sought a meaning for your life,' Bergman recalls, adding: 'You could soar up to the height of the sun and stretch your dreams into the heavens.' Kafka stood apart: 'What hindered your power? You were always left to your own devices, and so you found the strength to be alone.' His politics, too, retained their early, radical tinge in his later years, as evidenced by the seven-point programme he drew up in 1917–18 for a community of workers involving no private ownership.

Kafka enrolled at the German Charles Ferdinand University in Prague from 1901 until 1906, switching from chemistry to law, humanities (including literature and art), and finally back to law. The pattern of the solitary who seeks his own way already exhibits Kafka's typical equivocations and reversals, and the later conflict between his bourgeois

Václav Jansa (1859–1913): 'A Street in the Prague Ghetto', near the Old Town Square, from Jansa's cycle of paintings *Old Prague* (1899). Jansa was fascinated by Prague's heritage and devoted himself to preserving it. The picture shows the area close to Kafka's birthplace, at the time when he was about sixteen.

Václav Jansa: A painting from his cycle *Old Prague* (1899) showing the Old New Synagogue, Europe's oldest surviving synagogue (built around 1270), with the Jewish Town Hall (1680s; rebuilt 1763), where Kafka made two of his rare public appearances, lecturing on the Yiddish theatre in 1912, and reciting from Kleist's *Michael Kohlhaas* in 1913. The Town Hall now contains Prague's Jewish Museum.

profession and his vocation.

The university years also provided an entrée into literary life. Most importantly, in these his student years, Kafka made his first literary friends, and the circle of Prague German writers began to form that provided his immediate literary context. Along with other schoolfriends such as Bergman and Paul Kisch (elder brother of the future journalist Egon Erwin Kisch) in 1901 he joined the liberal-minded Reading and Lecture Hall of the German Students in Prague, where a distant cousin, Bruno Kafka, played a leading role. Kafka became an active member, attending and probably helping to organize cultural activities, notably readings and lectures. Another member was Oskar Pollak, who had replaced Bergman as his closest friend in his last years at school, and now became his 'window' on the world. It was a lively time in the Hall's literary life, not least thanks to Max Brod's participation: a major cycle of readings by local writers took place, and the celebrated German poet Detlev von Liliencron read twice (with Kafka forking out 10 Crowns towards his fee). By 1905, though, Kafka withdrew, probably to prepare for his exams, after having entered a vibrant literary scene.

Kafka's schoolfriend, Oskar Pollak (1883–1915). 'We have been talking together for three years. In some things I can no longer distinguish what's yours and what's mine ...' (Kafka to Pollak, 4 February 1902). Oskar Pollak later became an art historian. He was killed in action in the First World War.

Kafka's closest friend, the writer and critic Max Brod (1884–1968). At Brod's instigation, Kafka began his diaries, and disciplined himself as a writer. Brod's posthumous publication of his novels and stories made Kafka world-famous.

He was fortunate that his formative years fell during a local cultural efflorescence that itself coincided with the long moment of European modernism. Just as the national revival had heralded a new Czech literature, with figures like the writers Jan Neruda and Jaroslav Hašek, who was born the same year as Kafka, in the late nineteenth and early twentieth centuries a new Austrian literature emerged in Vienna and, most remarkably, in Prague, with poets like Hugo Salus, and the young Rilke. These latter writers were followed by the neoromantic Young Prague circle, including Paul Leppin and the early Expressionist Ludwig Hadwiger, the leading literary group before Max Brod appeared on the scene.

Kafka met Brod in 1902 when the latter lectured on Schopenhauer at the Reading and Lecture Hall, and probably that year also met the Louvre Circle centred on the philosopher, Franz Brentano, a link he loosely maintained until 1905, when Brod was excluded for allegedly satirizing Brentano in a novella. Other participants included several of Kafka's friends, among them Bergman, Pollak, Felix Weltsch, and Max and Berta Fanta, whose salon at 17 Old Town Square the circle also attended, and which Kafka visited from time to

Oskar Baum (1883–1941), one of Kafka's closest friends. Born partially sighted, he was blinded by a Czech child in a racially motivated attack. Educated as a musician, he established himself as a writer and critic in Prague.

Felix Weltsch (1884–1964), one of Kafka's closest friends. The fourth member of the Prague literary circle that included Kafka, Brod and Baum. Editor of the Zionist paper *Selbstwehr*, to which Kafka subscribed.

time until around 1914. Although Kafka did not attend regularly, disliking the Fanta salon, his closeness to the group is indicated by the fact that he and Oskar Pollak performed a satire on Brentano's philosophy at the Fantas' on New Year's Eve in 1904. Brentano's emphasis on 'self-analysis' and 'moral judgement' may have left a mark on his thought, apparent in an image of the kind that later formed the nodal point for his tales: 'We burrow into ourselves like a mole and return from our buried sandhills quite black and velvet-furred.' One thinker in this circle who particularly interested Kafka was Brentano's pupil, Christian von Ehrenfels, the founder of gestalt psychology. Another visitor was Albert Einstein. It seems likely that Kafka first encountered Freudian psychology and Einstein's Theory of Relativity here, as well as Ernst Mach's own, earlier

The interior of Café Arco, at the corner of Hibernergasse and Pflastergasse (Hybernská / Dlážděná), the best-known Prague literary café. From 1908 it included Kafka among its habitués, the 'Arconauts'. It was here that Kafka first encountered Franz Werfel, and met his future lover, the Czech journalist Milena Jesenská.

relativity theory. These ideas, including Mach's view that the belief in a stable 'personality' must be discarded, all left traces in Kafka's writing, and may be reflected in his earliest surviving prose work, *Description of a Struggle*, dating from 1904. The story indicates how deeply Kafka immersed himself in contemporary letters: lively evocations of Prague scenes observed after a party such as might have been held by the Fantas are juxtaposed with orientally inspired episodes and, as Klaus Wagenbach observes, the story even echoes the day's leading poets, refashioning a line by Stefan George. In Kafka's hands, George's melodious 'The fruits are knocking on the ground' becomes aggressive: 'The unripe fruit beat crazily on the ground.' The young Kafka is forging his own style, and in so doing measures himself against the contemporary greats.

Kafka's friends easily melded with the Prague café scene. The Young Prague group met at Café Renaissance, while Café Central was a favourite among younger writers, including Brod, Bergman, and Egon Erwin Kisch. From 1908, Café Arco became the central haunt for the Prague avant-garde, whom Karl Kraus mockingly christened the 'Arconauts'. Kafka's own circle began to form after 1903. This literary quartet was disparate enough to provide each of them with a powerful stimulus: Max Brod, the fluent young writer; Oskar Baum, the blind poet who overcame a childhood disability inflicted on him, a Jewish child, as supposed 'German' by a gang of Czech youths; Felix Weltsch, the rigorous thinker; and the shy, retiring Kafka, who at first preferred to conceal his own writing, and recite other authors' work.

Kafka's views in the early years, indebted to the Prague *fin-de-siècle* and the journal *Kunstwart*, are reflected in letters to Oskar Pollak. In 1902, Kafka still affects impressionism, as when describing the country idyll advocated by *Kunstwart* in terms of 'brown and melancholy' fields with their 'aban-

Charles Bridge (Karlsbrücke / Karlův most), linking the Old Town and the Lesser Town (Kleinseite/Mála Strana). Prague's oldest bridge, built in the Gothic style in 1357 by Peter Parler and later decorated with baroque statues, has always occupied a key place in the city's life, and is often mentioned by Kafka in his diaries, letters, stories and poems.

doned ploughs'. He continues: 'Have you already noticed how the late summer shadows dance on the ploughed earth?' His early verse, like Rilke's *Household Gods* (1896), celebrates the atmosphere associated with *Praga magica*, as in a poem that evokes Charles Bridge:

People, who walk across dark bridges,
past saints
with pale lights

František Drtikol (1883–1961): *Charles Bridge* (1912). The twilit, melancholic mood in Kafka's works has much in common with that captured by Drtikol and other Prague artists.

Clouds, that race across the grey skies
past churches
with twilit towers

A man, who leans on the ashlar parapet
and looks into the evening stream
his hands on the old stones.

The observer's pose is a favourite one in these years. Kafka recalls in his aphorisms, collected as *He*, how he stood on Prague's Petřín Hill (the German Laurenziberg), and formulated his main aim: 'to gain a view of life' in which life retains its 'natural heavy rise and fall', yet is 'simultaneously understood as a nothing, a mere dream ...'

Kafka's favourite books in the early phase – Adalbert Stifter's *Indian Summer* and Johan Peter Hebel's *Treasure Chest* – inculcated a lean, classical style, as did Friedrich Hebbel's diaries. Among the contemporary works which he encountered as they appeared was Thomas Mann's *Tonio Kröger*, published in 1903. Kafka identified with Mann's treatment of Tonio's artist-problem, which develops the dilemma presented in Goethe's *Torquato Tasso*, and from Tonio's resolution of the problem he learned how to appreciate 'the strange usefulness' of 'being in love with opposites'. His own, stern literary demands crystallized around this time, and in a letter of 27 January 1904, Kafka formulated the radical aesthetic which was to propel him into his major phase. As if transferring Nietzsche's credo, 'I am dynamite', to the artistic object, he writes:

I think we should only read books which bite and sting. If the book that we read doesn't wake us like a blow to the skull, why do we read the book? To make us happy ... ? My God, we could be happy even if we had no books, and if really necessary we could write books to make us happy ourselves. But we need the books that affect us like a disaster that hurts us greatly, like the death of someone we love

The Laurenziberg (Petřín) in Prague, which features prominently in *Description of a Struggle*, and is mentioned in Kafka's other writings. The tower was built in 1891 in imitation of the Eiffel Tower.

more dearly than ourselves, as if we were driven out into forests, far away from any human beings, like a suicide, a book must be the axe for the frozen sea within. That is what I believe.

Thus Kafka breaks through the 'beautiful semblance' demanded by German classical aesthetics, and formulates a violent poetics, appropriate to modernity. The dandy's pose that Kafka adopted in these years, seemingly at odds with this view, is just another variant on the theme of merging art with life, and increasingly, he fused them into one, to lend the same high visibility to his inner life as he did to his outer appearance. By this means, his writings depict an inner truth, and an often violent psychological reality.

Photographs support a friend's impression that Kafka was 'the best dressed man I ever met'. With pomaded hair, starched collars, and raffishly worn ties – albeit his right shoulder already droops from writing – Kafka in his twenties is style personified. And in his last year, when living in Berlin, Dora Dymant recalls how he

Drawings by Kafka. Probably after 1906. According to Brod, Kafka used to draw in his notebooks as a student, and Gustav Janouch relates that he continued 'this deeply ingrained habit' for many years, which provided him with a simple, direct means to express some of his major themes, from athleticism and dandyism to guilt and despair.

Kafka at the time of his graduation (1906).

would gaze at himself in the mirror before leaving the house. Though he could hardly afford a packet of butter, he was still dressed by the best tailor in town. He always knew what he looked like: 'I caused a bit of a stir,' he confessed once, 'with my crumpled soft hat in my hand ... ' The eyes which fix the camera are eyes which have learned to conquer.

As a boy, he recalled in 1922, he was as 'naïve and uninterested in sexual matters as I am, say, in relativity theory today', and resisted an attempt by a governess to seduce him. Later, he acquired that openness towards sexuality also evident in the novels. His account of how he lost his virginity, which he relates in a letter written in August 1920, is forthright. He begins playfully, but ends in trauma:

I remember the first night. We lived in Zeltnergasse [Celetná] then, opposite a clothiers; there was always a shop-girl standing in the door, I was upstairs, about 20 years old, constantly walking up and down in my room, busy with the nerve-racking activity of learning meaningless things for my first state exams. It was in the summer, very hot at the time, quite unbearable, I always stopped at the window, disgusting Roman legal history between my teeth, in the end we communicated by sign language. I was to collect her in the evening at 8 o'clock, but when I came down, someone else was there already, well, that didn't change much, I was afraid of the whole world, and so I was afraid of this man, too; even if he had not been there I would have still been afraid of him. But though the girl took his arm, she signalled that I should follow them. So we came to the Schützeninsel [Střelecký ostrov – an island in the Vltava], had a beer, I was at the neighbouring table, and then we slowly walked back to the girl's flat, I was trailing them, it was somewhere by the Meat Market [Fleischmarkt/Masný trh], the man said good-bye there, the girl ran into the house, I waited a little until she came outside again, and we went to a hotel in the Lesser Town [Kleinseite /Malá Strana]. All that, even before the hotel, was charming, exciting, and disgusting, and it was no different in the hotel. And then when we walked home in the morning over Charles Bridge, it was still warm and beautiful, I was really happy, but the happiness only consisted in the fact that I was finally left in peace by my body's constant complaints, but above all my happiness consisted in the fact that the whole thing had not been *more* disgusting, not *more* dirty ...

The episode becomes an anecdote, through which Kafka analyses the conjunction of sexuality and pollution, and so lends the occasion a formative meaning, which is more fully explored in *The Trial*, with its study of pollution and the sacred. His demands were absolute, and therefore tended to opposites. This bedevilled almost all his relationships, and his problems increased since, as he once confessed, he was inflamed by every girl he set eyes on. A brief affair with an older woman followed in 1905 while he was holidaying at a sanatorium in Zuckmantel (Zlaté Hory). Perhaps to renew the liaison, Kafka returned to the same place the following summer. By now he was a Doctor of Law, having graduated in Prague University's splendid Karolinum on 18 June 1906.

At the Workers' Accident Insurance

The real hell is in the office, I am not afraid of any other ...

To Felice

Kafka never wished to earn a living from literature, believing, according to Brod, that this would 'debase' his art. He was equally sceptical about journalism, and in later life refused to take on the editorship of a journal. Instead, he entered the world of normal work. From 1906 to 1907, he did his practical as a lawyer, and on 1 October 1907 took a job in an Austro-Italian insurance company, *Assicurazioni Generali*. With typical self-mockery, he plays the part of a desk-bound Rimbaud:

My life now is completely disorderly. However I do have a job, with a tiny salary of 80 Crowns, and 8–9 endless working hours; but I devour the hours outside the office like a wild animal. Because I was not used to limiting my normal life to six hours a day, and I'm learning Italian, too, and want to spend the evenings of these very lovely days in the open, I return hardly refreshed at all from my busy free time.

Building of the Arbeiter-Unfall-Versicherungs-Anstalt für das Königreich Böhmen (Workers' Accident Insurance Company of the Kingdom of Bohemia), Pořič 7 (Na Poříčí). Kafka's office lay on the top floor. On the left (beside the hotel), a cinema he frequented, Grande Théâtre Bio Elite.

I ... hope to sit on a chair in a very distant land one day, and see the sugar cane fields from my office windows, or see the Muslim cemeteries. I find the insurance business very interesting, but my work at the moment is miserable.

He lasted only briefly in this tedious, all-consuming job – it no doubt contributed to the image of the office in *The Trial*, where Joseph K.'s boss speaks Italian, and his own knowledge of the language is put to the test at a meeting with an Italian client – and he left after three-quarters of a year. Then, on 30 July 1908, he started as a temporary assistant at the Workers' Accident Insurance Company of the Kingdom of Bohemia, located at Na Poříčí 7, and stayed there for his entire working life. In 1910 he became an articled clerk, in 1913 he was promoted to Vice Secretary, in 1920 to Company Secretary, and in 1922 to Senior Secretary before being pensioned off for health reasons. The company provided more congenial conditions and better suited his political leanings, having been established as a public corporation under the aegis of the State after the enactment of the Austrian Workers' Accident Law of 1887. In Kafka's day, the Prague office, which employed 200 people, was the most important in the Empire. Every business with twenty employees or more was required to be insured, and in 1911 the Prague office wrote the policies for 288,094 enterprises, i.e. 46.79% of all the businesses in Austria (i.e. the Empire excluding Hungary). This represented one-third of Austria's total industrial capacity. Kafka thus acquired a precise inside knowledge of the ways in which the twentieth-century's defining trends – modernization, industrialization, and mechanization – worked themselves out in practice. Similarly, he had to grapple with the era's major issues relating to the conflict between workers and capital. Questions concerning government, administration, bureaucracy, and the law were fundamental to his work. This practical knowledge, and specific questions

Dr Robert Marschner, Director of the Workers' Accident Insurance Company, with his daughter Berta, who once appeared in a macabre dream of Kafka's and 'as I recently noticed, is on the way to becoming a fat, stiffly dressed little girl ...' (*Diaries*, 2 October 1911).

concerning danger, risk, and accidents, reappear – transmuted, estranged, transcended – in his major writings. Justice, the law, and bureaucracy provide him with key themes in his first major phase, and danger is all-pervasive in his work: Gregor Samsa's transformation, Joseph K.'s arrest, the uncontrollable machine of *In the Penal Colony* – Kafka's world is under constant threat, defined by risk and the damage caused by a single accident.

Kafka's superiors went some way towards mitigating the job's unpleasantness, making his 'double life' as bearable as possible. He appreciated 'the heartfelt social feeling' of the Director, Robert Marschner, who shared his literary interests: 'Recently,' he told Felice in 1912, 'we were head to head in his office in a book of Heine's poetry while in the ante-room servants, office heads, and clients were waiting impatiently to be admitted.' He also much admired the Head of his Department, Eugen Pfohl, of whom he wrote that he 'gives me strength', being a model to 'imitate'. Only the President of the Council, Otto Příbram, whose appearance reminded him of Kaiser Franz Josef, sometimes caused him problems, ever since once in 1911 – as he relates in a letter of January 1913 – Kafka burst out into uncontrollable laughter in

The Johann Liebig Woollen Goods Factory at Reichenberg (Liberec), the centre of the industrial region in northern Bohemia. Along with three other manufacturing towns, Reichenberg belonged to Kafka's remit as an insurance official, which involved him in many business trips. Other factories here produced glass, machines, and automobiles.

his presence. However, his superiors appreciated Kafka's excellence.

He was active in several departments, dealing with issues like pensions, statistics, risk assessment, and accident prevention. Because of his 'excellent drafting skills', he also contributed to the annual reports, and acted as a speech-writer, thereby gaining an overview of the whole enterprise. His first mature writings were actually official documents, and if their style accommodates to legal and administrative requirements, their clarity, fluency, and vividness set them apart from the usual bureaucratic documents. In 1908, not long after starting the job, his report 'On the extent of the obligation to insure in the building trade and in related trades' delineates the stark conflicts faced by his organization and their somewhat unlikely resolution. The conflicts he faced between employers and workers are not dissimilar to those found in his later writing, but in these early

professional texts, he still envisages an ideal form of conflict resolution:

A possible source for Kafka's novel, the castle in Friedland (Frýdlant), northern Bohemia. The factory in the foreground, which produced fine cloth, was overseen by Kafka, who spent an extended period working in Friedland in January–February 1911. The castle, once owned by Wallenstein, belonged to the Counts Clam-Gallas, a name echoed in that of Klamm, the official in *The Castle*.

When the interests of the workers (the protection of as many workers as possible, compensation for as many accidents as possible) and the interests of the employers (the lowest possible contributions shared equitably among as many employers as possible) are met, the interests of the organization will be met.

His hope was that an 'authentic interpretation of the law will restore order'. However, this ideal was very far from the reality, in which the law was often wrong, misapplied, and incomprehensible. In fact, the situation that Kafka encountered in the insurance organization provided a starting-point for the grotesque reality described in *The Trial*, where the law is similarly obscure, and lacks any 'authentic interpretation'.

Kafka's work involved him travelling widely in Bohemia as a risk assessor, or defending the organization's position to disgruntled businessmen. The industries that he engaged with were at the forefront of technological progress, including the newly emerging automotive industry, timber working, and quarrying. Indeed, an understanding of new technology was so important that in 1909 he attended lectures – during working hours – at Prague's Technical University to enable him to judge objections to his classification of risk categories. The precise technical insight into mechanization and its discontents that he obtained at university and at work fused with his

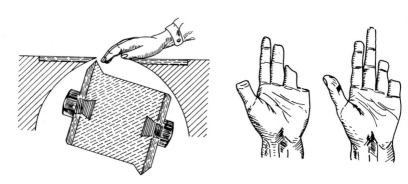

Illustrations from Kafka's *Accident Prevention for Wood-Planing Machines* (1909) showing the dangers of a rectangular plane revolving at 3,000– 4,000 rpm. As Kafka explains, accidents involving 'the loss of several finger bones, or even entire fingers' could be prevented by using circular 'safety planes'.

own, personal fascination with machines – one summer, he delighted in the novelty of motor-cycling in the country – and is evident in the telephones, trams, and automobiles that figure so widely in his writing. Indeed, coming to terms with machines was formative in helping him to develop his own, appropriately modernistic style.

The electrification of Bohemia's saw-mills, which employed 80,000 workers, caused many accidents, and Kafka was instrumental in pushing through major reforms: 'Who has a

magic hand,' he asks in his diary, 'that he can place into a machine without it being torn and tossed aside by a thousand knives?' Speaking to Max Brod about the pathetic injured workers, Kafka commented: 'How

Kafka aged twenty-seven. In 1912 he sent this picture to his fiancée, Felice Bauer, adding: 'I don't actually have a twisted face, I only have a visionary gaze when taken with a flash, and I stopped wearing high collars a long time ago. However, the suit is my only one, the one I have often mentioned before (only one is exaggerated, but not very), and I wear it today as cheerfully as I did then. It ages with me.'

modest these people are. They come to us with requests. Instead of storming the company and smashing everything to bits they come with requests...' Here, and in the unfortunate asbestos business venture in which his family involved him, Kafka witnessed the massive pain, suffering, and dehumanization inflicted by industrialization. In a single, long sentence in his diaries, he summarizes the fate of countless girls:

Yesterday in the factory. The girls are not human beings in their unbearably dirty and loose clothes, with their hair in disarray as if they had just woken up, with the unchanging expressions on their faces, here amid the continuous noise of the transmissions and the machines, which work automatically but break down unpredictably, nobody greets anyone, nobody apologizes if they bump into the girls, if someone calls them over to perform a small task they will do it, but then go straight back to the machine, where someone indicates where to help by a toss of the head, they stand about in their underwear, and are completely at the mercy of even the smallest power, without even enough clear reason to acknowledge that power with their eyes or by a bow ...

The insight into such demeaning experiences in Central Europe's most advanced industrial region shortly fed directly into Kafka's literary portrayal of mechanized suffering in his first extant novel, *The Lost One* (*America*).

His 'double life' put Kafka under severe strain, as the office inevitably collided with his vocation. As early as 1910, at an appointment with Rudolf Steiner, the founder of anthroposophy (a form of theosophy), Kafka explained: ' ... these two professions can never tolerate one another. The smallest happiness in the one becomes a great unhappiness in the other.' A year later, he records his physical collapse: 'I am simply overworked. Not just from the office, but from my other work.' Suicide was often on his mind: 'A single shot would be the best.'

The Making of a Writer

Hold fast to your diary from today! Write regularly! Don't give yourself up! Even if no salvation comes, I want to be worthy of it at any moment.

Kafka, *Diaries*

In the crucial years leading up to his first major phase, the problematic but ultimately productive tension that Kafka experienced between the office and his writing was deepened by further dichotomies, which, incidentally, reflected Prague's geographical position as a meeting point between east and west. On the one hand, he felt drawn to the modernizing, western world, with its proliferating materialism and popular pleasures; whilst on the other, he was increasingly attracted to the archaic religion of his forebears,

Joke photograph of Kafka with the writers Albert Ehrenstein and Otto Pick and the Zionist Lize Kaznelson at the Prater, the Viennese amusement park, 1913. Kafka was in Vienna for a conference on accident prevention, and also used the opportunity to visit the eleventh Zionist Congress.

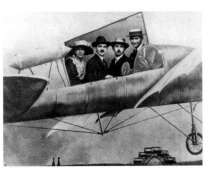

and a spirituality that he associated with the east. The two tendencies meet in his own, inimitable style, which combines two historical currents: firstly, the modernizing elements formulated in the late nineteenth-century empiricism he encountered during his studies; and, secondly, the Talmudic 'dialectics', fashioned by the rabbis in their biblical commentaries, that aimed to elaborate the Hebrew law in its application to every possible eventuality. Even among assimilated families like the Kafkas, with no direct training in the Talmud, its habits survived in their often gruff, ironically adversarial speech (which so upset the young Kafka in his father), and (as one visitor to the family noted) their obsession with retailing and analysing every experience. Kafka united these different traits in a literary medium which is based on the living, spoken language used by the Prague German bourgeoisie, which was famous for its linguistic correctness and grammatical accuracy. The result is a style that, whilst open to modernist experimentation, is exemplary in its lucid, balanced classicism. Ultimately, Kafka learned to treat every word as a sign, signalling looks, gestures, movements, until his personality fully expressed itself in a peculiarly supple, almost seismographic way of writing.

Kafka's diaries – actually journals, notebooks, and dreambooks, which he kept from 1909 until shortly before his death – were the private refuge where he developed his personality. In his reading, he was particularly interested in autobiographical works such as Marcus Aurelius' meditations, Flaubert's letters and Goethe's diaries. In his own development during the early office years, when he remained outwardly unproductive, his diaries provided the magic mirror by which he transformed experience into art. Many apparently autobiographical statements prove to be *études de style*.

Encounters with curious individuals like the art collector and sex fiend A. M. Pachinger, who terrorized women with his 'enormous member', turn ineluctably into polished pen-portraits. Other entries recount dreams, as when – in one typical mechanistic nightmare – he sees a blind child, who resembles his boss's little daughter, and whose glasses are attached by a lever inserted into her cheekbone. In such visions, the inner life assumes an overpowering force, vying with empirical fact, and initiates the alchemy by which Kafka fused actual experiences with dreams and fantasies to create literature. One fantasy, in which he imagines being sliced up like a sausage, reads like a macabre anecdote. Another, from 1911, reappears at the end of *The Trial*: 'This morning for the

Max Brod. Lithograph by the Czech artist Willi Nowak (1911). Kafka was present when Nowak showed this portrait to Brod and explained his working methods (*Diaries*, 23 December 1911).

first time in a long while I took pleasure again in the idea of a knife being turned in my heart.' In 1914, this nightmare world became paramount: 'The represen-tation of my dream-like inner world has pushed everything else into second place.' Constantly, too, the diaries stress Kafka's isola-tion, frustration, and despair, 'the terrible uncer-tainty of my inner exis-tence.'

His inner solitude notwithstanding, Kafka depended on friendship. After Hugo Bergman and Oskar Pollak, Brod for some years constituted his

The Gothic Powder Tower (Pulverturm/Prašná brána), erected in 1475, a former entrance to Prague. Brod and Kafka met here after work to walk home together. Kafka was generally late.

essential double. With Brod, he could share the maximum number of interests. For example, on the night they met, they discussed Hugo von Hofmannsthal's seminal text, *A Letter* (1901), which defines the crisis of language that typified the era. Brod regularly read his latest work to Kafka, who admired his writing, and relations grew close. In 1907–8, inspired by Kafka's enthusiasm for his French literary 'blood relative', they read Flaubert together in the original, over the years working their way through *L'éducation sentimentale*, *La tentation de saint Antoine*, and *Bouvard et Pécuchet*. By 1911, Kafka notes being 'almost completely under Max's influence'. They would meet after work (Brod had a job in the Post Office), or go on weekend outings, and also made several journeys together. However, in 1912, after Brod's engagement, when Kafka became involved with Felice Bauer and needed more time to write, a change set in: 'Max does not understand me,' he complained to Felice, 'and where he does, he is mistaken.' None the less, Brod remained Kafka's closest friend until the end.

Brod effected Kafka's introduction to literary life, and probably to Prague's night-life, too. Kafka himself had a keen eye for the age's major trends. In 1911 he attended readings by the leading Viennese intellectuals, Karl Kraus and Adolf Loos, who used the occasion to present their most important ideas, and also heard lectures by Rudolf

A drawing by Kafka entitled *Supplicant and Noble Patron*.

Steiner and Albert Einstein. Thus, intellectually, Kafka's Prague was close to Wittgenstein's Vienna. Kafka also subscribed to a key German literary journal, *Die Neue Rundschau*, and through Brod encountered the leading Expressionist journal *Die Aktion* (which, on occasion, he read avidly).

Kafka also continued to frequent Prague's literary cafés, such as the Arco, and was no stranger to its wine cellars and night-clubs. In his first years at work, he often went out on the town. But he was not really much of a drinker. His letters include only occasional references to beer and champagne, and later he abstained altogether, even avoiding tea and coffee. He was often a solitary guest. In one amusing anec-dote, he refers to just such a night at one of these 'wonderful places', probably the Trocadero, an expensive wine bar: the company comprised 'officers, Berliners, Frenchmen, painters, singers'. He concludes with a typically absurd detail: 'Because I didn't have anything for a tip, I lent the conductor of the orchestra a book instead.' To Brod, he also jokingly proposed replac-ing a costly night's drink-ing by an affordable morning-after:

... in the empty office I have had an almost excellent idea, which would be very cheap to execute. Instead of our usual night-life from Monday to Tues-day we could institute a pretty morning life, meeting at the Maria Statue at 5.30 – there'll be no lack of women then – and go to the Trocadero or to Chuchle or to the Eldorado. We

Kafka around 1906–8 with the waitress Hansi Julie Szokoll. According to Brod the liaison made Kafka very unhappy. Joseph K. has a similar link to a girl 'who worked at night as a waitress in a wine-bar until the early hours ...' (*The Trial*, Chapter 1).

could do as we pleased and drink a coffee in the garden by the Moldau [Vltava] or leaning on Josci's shoulders. Either would be pretty good. We wouldn't look bad in the Trocadero; there are millionaires and even richer folk who have no more money at six in the morning, and we would arrive ... just to drink a tiny coffee ... and have two girls for breakfast ...

Brod's diary confirms these amusements: 'Trocadero. He's in love with the Germania on the German postage stamps. *Chambre séparée*. But he is so strangely withdrawn. When he says: I'll pay for your apartment – he laughs, as if he meant it ironically.' At one time, Kafka entered a brief, unhappy liaison with the 'artiste' Hansi Szokoll, who he observed 'had been ridden over by entire cavalry regiments'. She reappears perhaps in the fictional Elsa, whom Joseph K. visits in *The Trial*.

The Munich-born chansonette Thea Degen (1911), whom Kafka saw perform at Cabaret Lucerna in 1912.

The diaries also record visits to brothels like the celebrated U Šuhů in Benediktgasse (Benediktská), mentioned in Hašek's *The Good Soldier Švejk*. In such observations – at work, in factories, cafés, brothels – experience elides with art:

The three little doors that lead from the interior of the building into the salon. The guests

as if onstage in a waxworks. The drinks on the table, hardly touched. The flat-faced one in the corner in the angular dress, which only starts to move very low down in the hem. Some of them here and before are dressed like marionettes for a children's theatre, like the ones sold at the Christmas market with loosely sewn ruches and gold stuck on ...

Konsul Peter, who performed at Prague's Théâtre Variété in Karolinental (Karlín) in 1908–9, and was a prototype for Red Peter in *A Report for an Academy*.

As in the factory, Kafka observes how modern woman has become a commodity, whereby life loses any authentic value.

Cabaret and popular entertainment fascinated him. He records seeing the chansonette, Thea Degen, to whom his friend Werfel dedicated an ecstatic poem in 1913, and Gusti Odys, who danced the seven veils: 'Stiff hips. Really fleshless. Red knees only good for dancing "Spring Mood".' Another belle was Mella Mars, whom Kafka watched in Cabaret Lucerna: 'A witty tragedian ... she has a tired, but very flat, empty

Georges Seurat: *Le Cirque* (1891). Seurat's celebrated, unfinished painting inspired kafka's later story, *From the Gallery*.

'I...quickly walked on, more and more people followed me...I couldn't find my way...' An illustration by Alfred Kubin for his fantastic novel *The Other Side* (1908), which foretells the end of civilization in mass destruction via the story of a 'dream kingdom' governed by an inscrutable, irrational system. The motif is echoed in *The Trial* and *The Castle*.

face ... She speaks very sharply and her movements seem to start from her upturned thumb, which seems to be made of strong sinew, not bones. Her nose is particularly changeable in the changing lights ... ' When Kafka was sick, he had to miss one such evening, but Brod visited the Lucerna with his wife, and reported the events to him at length.

Artistry, acrobatics, and gymnastics all play a part in the early works: Karl, the hero of *The Lost One*, enters a kind of circus; Georg, the hero of *The Judgement*, becomes a gymnast in the hour of his death; and Gregor, in *The Metamorphosis*, enjoys his new-found acrobatic freedom, climbing around the ceiling. Indeed, as with the art of the École de Paris – one thinks of Toulouse-Lautrec, Seurat, and Picasso – cabaret, operetta, circus artistes and *variété* not only contribute details and local colour to Kafka's

work, but provide the subject for the later tales, which re-orientate the traditional

A drawing by Kafka of a runner, exhibiting the typical wavy lines of the art nouveau style, and the contemporary fascination with speed. It was probably done between 1901–6.

handling of the artist figure from Goethe's *Tasso* to Mann's *Tonio Kröger* by depicting the artist as a performance artiste.

Whereas Kafka did not consider himself to be musical – a view one must relativize by attending to the musicality of his prose, which he himself stressed, and to his musical manner of recitation – the visual arts greatly affected him. *From the Gallery*, for example, transposes Seurat's *Le Cirque* into a symbolic anecdote. Perhaps the artist who most influenced Kafka was the Moravian draughtsman, Alfred Kubin, whom he met in 1911. Kubin's drawings and etchings, deriving from the symbolist nightmares of Redon and Ensor, develop a macabre vision, which provides a model for Kafka's own grotesque imagery: although Kubin's mixing of human and animal forms may possibly have contributed to the inspiration for *The Metamorphosis*, it is above all the mood Kubin generates by depicting absurd images in an *angst*-ridden world which provides the key comparison: in one drawing, a

The Murakami Truppe

A troupe of Japanese Murakami acrobats of the kind that performed in Prague's Théâtre Variété in Karolinental (Karlín) in November 1909.

man rides upon a giant wave mounted on a tiny bicycle, as if lost in the cosmic void; in another, a man (who almost seems to anticipate K.) treks through a barren landscape, overlooked by two enormous, brooding birds. 'Perhaps I will one day manage to say,' Kafka wrote to Kubin, 'what your work means to me.' The nineteenth century's fascination with shadowy darknesses, exemplified in Doré's Paris and Dickens's London, and which contributed to the birth of photography, seems to have lingered on in Prague. Kafka's own imaginings were also much enriched by the moving image. The first cinema opened in Prague in 1907, and Kafka became an avid viewer of such 'utter rubbish' as *The White Slave Girl*. He enjoyed acting out comic 'cinematographic' episodes, and in his first major phase, adapted his inner visions to cinematic convention, notably in *The Trial*, which is typified by a brooding, monochromatic imagination. Kafka's own drawings also belong in this ambiance. 'I was a great draughtsman once,' he wrote to Felice in 1913, 'those drawings satisfied me more than anything else.' Representing what he felt and saw, as in the dramatic sketch of the Japanese acrobats who played at Prague's Théâtre Variété, his drawings develop from a curvaceous *Jugendstil* manner, but then tend to a cursive Expressionism – distantly recalling Kubin and Klee – in several desperate hieroglyphs, which construct the human body around the letter 'K'. These images employ the same cultural iconography as the Czech avant-garde photographer, František Drtikol, noted both for his evocative Prague courtyard scenes and for his erotica, in which the human body is captured as a stark calligraphic unit casting a vivid, spiritual shadow.

The obverse to the aesthete's pose that Kafka adopted in these years, equally focused on bodily prowess, was that of the naturist, a practical interest in nudity which converged with that in Czech and German Symbolist art around 1900. Walking, hiking, swimming, riding, cycling, rowing, gymnastics, nudism – all these were pursuits that Kafka engaged in. Some were typical for the

A drawing by Kafka: '… Japanese acrobats, who climb onto a ladder which does not rest on the ground, but on the soles of someone else's feet who is semi-recumbent, and which does not lean on the wall, but goes up into the air. I can't do that …' (*Diaries*, November/December 1909).

František Drtikol: *Surprise* (1927). Kafka's aesthetic trajectory resembled that of Czech artists like Drtikol, developing the symbolism into magical realism and treating human figures like 'K.' as a kind of hieroglyphic cipher.

A drawing by Kafka of a jockey, reflecting his new, expressionistic style, and the interest in horse racing he developed after taking up riding in 1909–10.

early modern German return to nature, as in the German youth movement, and others more specifically for the development of what was perceived as a 'healthy' German national identity. In Kafka's case, the identity emancipated by these activities was purely his own. In his perception, his body – he was nearly six foot tall – was useless, assembled from a 'junk room'. He complained about his lankiness, his thinness, his weak heart. What the Germans called 'body culture' was therefore essential practical training, in that it helped to unify him as a living being and so turn him into an appropriate literary 'instrument'. As a swimmer, for example, he could compete with his father and, by swimming, he lost his embarrassment at his own body. Just as modern psychology enabled him to effect a new grasp of the mind, body culture assisted him in creating anew his own identity, untouched by his parents, exclusive to his own person, supposedly unaffected by the city and close to nature, and independent of tradition.

The holistic view of the self as an athletic object physically acting in space and possessed of elastic mental attributes ultimately provides the basis for Kafka's grasp of character. In his writing, from early images like the obese Buddha in *Description of a Struggle* or Brunelda in *The Lost One*, Kafka's engagement with the body matures, and the stories indicate how he increasingly divested himself of embarrassment. Throughout his work, the human subject is unimaginable without the cut of its clothes, and its own, naked skin.

The Breakthrough

This is the only way to write ... with this complete opening of body and soul ...

Kafka, *Diaries*

Several journeys crucially extended Kafka's personality and helped precipitate his literary breakthrough. In 1909, as Brod relates, they travelled to Italy. They read of a forthcoming Air Meet: 'We had never seen an aeroplane before ... Kafka particularly wanted to make the expedition.' The result was one of Kafka's earliest publications, *The Aeroplanes in Brescia*, which appeared in a Prague German paper that very month. With wit and wonder, Kafka conjures up the crowd, the aviators, the engine problems, and the brilliant flight of an aeroplane, its wings 'shining in the sun'. The fascination

Die Aeroplane in Brescia.
Von Franz Kafka (Prag).

Wir sind angekommen. Vor dem Aerobrom liegt noch ein großer Platz mit verdächtigen Holzhäuschen, für die wir andere Aufschriften erwartet hätten, als: Garage, Grand Büfett International und so weiter. Ungeheure in ihren Wägelchen fettgewordene Bettler strecken uns ihre Arme in den Weg, man ist in der Eile versucht, über sie zu springen. Wir überholen viele Leute und werden von vielen überholt. Wir schauen in die Luft, um die es sich hier ja handelt. Gott sei Dank, noch fliegt keiner! Wir weichen nicht aus und werden doch nicht überfahren. Zwischen und hinter den Tausend Fuhrwerken und ihnen entgegen hüpft italienische Kavallerie. Ordnung und Unglücksfälle scheinen gleich unmöglich.

The opening of Kafka's *The Aeroplanes in Brescia* (1909), the first essay on aeronautics in German literature.

Two planes described in *The Aeroplanes in Brescia*. *In the oval*: Louis Blériot in flight past the stands at Brescia. *Main picture*: a Curtiss flyer, with which Curtiss won the Brescia Grand Prix, with a flight of 50 kilometres in 49 min. 24 sec.

with planes brought the two friends into the ambit of Italian Futurism, then the most advanced artistic movement in Europe, which was inspiring the avant-garde all the way from Mayakovski's Moscow to the Paris of Apollinaire and the London of Pound and Lewis. Marinetti's *Futurist Manifesto* had appeared in *Le Figaro* in Paris in 1909. The parallels, if not necessarily the influence, can be seen in the Futurist 'free-word' style adopted in Brod's Paris diary of 1909–11, and also in the subjects of Kafka's notes that record his own Paris trips – including one in 1910, the *annus mirabilis* of modernism – during which he encountered modernity at its most vibrant. In 1910 the two friends stayed at Hôtel Windsor, 26 rue de Saint-Pétersbourg and in 1911 at Hôtel Sainte

Marie, 83 rue Rivoli. Experiences whirled by on boulevards and the métro, in cafés, bars, restaurants, theatres, cinemas, variety shows, popular entertainments (when Kafka astounded Brod by his acrobatics in ascending a rope), as well as at the Louvre, and, of course, at a French brothel (from which Kafka fled!). A little poem in French that Kafka jotted down indicates his open, all-seeing attitude:

Moi je flâne
Qu'on m'approuve ou me condamme
Je vois tout
Je suis partout.

Towards the end of Kafka's Paris diary, he seems to parody Marinetti's slogan: 'A speeding car is more beautiful than Nike of Samothrace.' The two motifs in Marinetti's dictum – the sculpture and the car – appear in two separate entries in Kafka's diary. In the first, he describes the Venus de Milo, but does so dynamically, in a Futurist way. In the second – the longest piece he wrote in Paris – he describes an automobile, but instead of seeing it futuristically as a speeding object, he describes a car crash. Kafka continues this debate with Futuristic themes in his first novel, *The Lost One*, which starts with a chapter called 'The Stoker'. This is one of the very themes that Marinetti advocated to his contemporaries. However, Kafka's concerns are ultimately at odds with Futurism. He moved away from it later in his career, concentrating on what he regarded as the deeper source of works like *The Lost One*, namely what he calls an 'inner truth'.

In 1911, a Yiddish theatre troupe that performed in Prague until early 1912 attracted his notice. Through its performances, and especially through the person of its leading actor, Jizchak Löwy, Kafka first encountered a living

Overleaf Rue du Louvre, Paris. 'It is easier to steer a car on asphalt, but more difficult to stop it ...' Kafka was fascinated by the traffic in streets like this, where he witnessed a car crash.

Jewish culture. This proved crucial. In eastern Judaism, he discovered his own religious 'origins', believing it would 'enlighten' his hitherto 'lethargic Judaism'. Like Chagall, Kafka found a vital inspiration in eastern Jewish folklore. Through Löwy, he discovered the Yiddish language and its literature, and heard about the Talmud, which codifies Jewish law, as well as about the very different mystical tradition contained in the Zohar, 'the Bible of the Kabbalists'. He was particularly drawn to the culture of the Hassidim, with their magical legends surrounding the famous Wonder Rabbis. He thus implicitly reached back to the magi-

Kafka's friend, the Yiddish actor Jizchak Löwy (1887–1942) in the role of the Wild Man by Jakob Gordin, performed in Prague, 1911. Born in Warsaw, Löwy became an actor in Paris, and joined a travelling theatre. He later returned to Poland and lived in the Warsaw Ghetto under the Nazi occupation. He was killed in Treblinka.

cal Prague that had been physically destroyed with the Ghetto. This culture is epitomized in the stories surrounding the great Rabbi Löw, who was said to have given life to a clay robot, the Golem, to perform his menial tasks, but who then ran amok, until Rabbi Löw destroyed him by effacing the kabbalistic signs on his clay forehead. The Yiddish theatre, which performed in cafés and similar smaller venues with relatively confined spaces, provided Kafka with a model for the perspectival foreshortenings and brilliant gestural language in his first great story, *The Judgement*, and even the *donnée* of *The Trial* – the arrest by two officials of an innocent man – can be traced back to a Yiddish play.

Meanwhile, Max Brod had begun to engineer Kafka's literary career. In 1906 they jointly subscribed to Franz Blei's literary periodical, *Der Amethyst*, and two years later Brod used the opportunity of a book review on Blei to slip in a reference to his wholly unknown friend, who, he claimed, belonged to a 'sacred group' of writers – Blei, Heinrich Mann, Meyrink, and Wedekind – which represented the 'noble culture of German letters'. Probably at Brod's instigation, too, Kafka reviewed a book by Blei. Shortly afterwards, in 1908, the latter gave a reading in Prague. The next year, he returned, Kafka collected him from the station, and in the evening they climbed the Laurenziberg, to view Halley's Comet. The literary courtship served Kafka well. In 1908, Blei became Kafka's first editor, bringing out his earliest publications – eight texts under the heading *Meditation* – in his yearbook, *Hyperion*. Others followed in newspapers.

Then, in July 1912, while on sick leave, Kafka travelled to Leipzig with Brod. In a café, in the company of other writers, including Walter Hasenclever and Kurt Pinthus, the future editor of the celebrated Expressionist anthology, *Menschheitsdämmerung* (*Twilight of Humanity*), Brod introduced him to the publisher Ernst Rowohlt,

Kafka's sketch of Goethe's garden house in Weimar, which he visited in the summer of 1912. Travelling to Weimar, the centre of German culture, and colonizing it in his own, whimsical manner by a flirtation with the daughter of the Goethe House custodian, may have helped to precipitate Kafka's literary breakthrough that autumn.

The writers Walter Hasenclever, Franz Werfel and Kurt Pinthus in Leipzig, 1912, around the time that Kafka met them there.

and his partner, Kurt Wolff. As if 'by chance', Kafka's first book was agreed. Notwithstanding his protests to Brod and his anguish over his 'poor work', by early August Kafka had compiled *Meditation*, and in December Rowohlt published it in an edition of 800 numbered copies. In some ways a typical art nouveau 'slim volume', the miniatures in *Meditation* – on such themes as bachelorhood and despair – contain much that is typical for Kafka. Even his style of presenting reality relativistically is already apparent in a short piece, *The Trees*:

For we are like tree-trunks in the snow. Apparently they lie there smoothly, and could easily be pushed away. No, you cannot do that, because they are firmly bound to the earth. But look, that too is only apparent.

A sense of unreality pervades this piece, whose lightness recalls Kafka's wish, formulated on the Laurenziberg, to capture life's 'rise and fall', and yet to treat it as 'a mere dream ...'

Meanwhile, the break-through had occurred. In a single night in September 1912, Kafka wrote *The Judgement* 'in a single stroke', or 'breath'. He

The house at the corner of Niklasstrasse (Mikulášská/modern Pařížská), where the family lived from 1907–15, and in which Kafka wrote *The Judgement* and *The Metamorphosis*: 'I call the street "a runway for suicides" because it leads straight to the river ...' (To Hedwig Weiler, 1908). The site is now occupied by Hotel InterContinental.

straightaway read it to his sisters, Valli and Ottla, and next day to Oskar Baum. Having drawn a line under the text in his

Niklas Brücke (Čechův most), built in 1906–8, with a view of Prague Castle in the distance. The Kafkas' apartment overlooked the bridge, which features in *The Judgement*.

diary, he adopts a telegraphic style to explain the way he wrote the story, indicating the precise, intensely physical mode of composition:

I wrote this story 'the Judgement' in the night of 22 to 23 from ten in the evening until six in the morning at a single stroke. I could hardly draw my legs, which had grown tired by being seated, from under the desk. The terrible strain and the joy as the story developed before me, and as it progressed through the waters. Often at night I carried my whole weight on my back. How everything can be ventured, how a strange fire is ready for all ideas, however strange, in which they burn up and are resurrected. How the light turned blue before my window. A carriage passed. Two men walked across the bridge. At 2 o'clock I looked at my watch for the last time. As the maid walked through the hall for the first time I wrote down the final sentence. Putting out the lamp and daybreak. The faint pains in my heart. The weariness that disappeared in the middle of the night.

The trembling entrance into my sisters' room. Reading aloud. Before that, stretching myself in the presence of the maid, and saying 'I was writing until now'. The appearance of my undisturbed bed, as though it had just been carried in ... This is the only way to write, only in such continuity, with this complete opening of body and soul ...

For the first time, Kafka had found a plot, centred on the archetypal conflict between father and son, in which the rational world is increasingly overtaken by the irrational, and the narrative is united by a single, dominant metaphor – in this case, the legal image of a judgement, which is exercised by the parent within the moral sphere, and enacted by the child in a totally unexpected suicide – death by drowning.

Allegorical figures of Victory on Niklas Brücke (Čechův most), which Kafka would have seen from his window. Similar allegories appear in *The Lost One* and *The Trial*.

The story's realistic setting is based on the Kafka family apartment in Niklasstrasse (Mikulášská), overlooking the new bridge across the river – the kind of plausible milieu that entered Czech fiction in Jan Neruda's *Prague Tales*. The characters involve what Kafka called 'a walk around' his family, and the central conflict both incorporates and transforms various biographical facts. Yet *The Judgement* defamiliarizes the realistic details, and the story takes on a threatening, grotesque character. The central theme, the father–son relationship, was a major one among Expressionists such as Franz Werfel and Walter Hasenclever, whose play *The Son* appeared in 1914, and the psychology was highly topical, too: Kafka's diary records his 'thoughts of Freud' on completing the story. However, by using the uncanny to probe beneath the surface, it reaches down into myth, recalling older versions of the theme, such as Abraham's intended sacrifice of Isaac in the Bible, the Greek *Oedipus*, and the ancient German narrative poem, *The Lay of Hildebrand*. As a result, *The Judgement* is as shocking as any tragedy, yet as richly textured and mysterious as any modern poem that 'cannot be explained'.

At last, Kafka had found a way of writing which fulfilled his aesthetic, formulated long before in the letter to Oskar Pollak, by baring the 'wound' in his conscience. Indeed, *The Judgement* focalizes all the sundry forces that Kafka contended with – the family, sexuality, business, writing – and subsumes them under a conflict, both pursued and judged by the father, between the hero's western world, and the eastern sphere, represented by the hero's double, the mysterious friend in Russia. The west means materialism in all its forms, both publicly in success in business – distantly evoking capitalism – and privately in sexual gratification. The east evokes asceticism, religion, and – by a mere allusion – political revolution. Via his hero's death, like Tonio Kröger, the writer learns to renounce a part of himself and to 'die' as a man in order to become an artist. Years later, he actually traced the origin of his tubercular 'wound' to this eruptive inspiration. The story appeared the next year in *Arcadia*, a yearbook edited by Brod for which Kafka had suggested the name.

This inspired tale, which exorcizes the contradictions in Kafka's personality, made him feel the unworthiness of the novel that he had started in the winter of 1911–12, presumably the first draft of *The Lost One*, and he began the surviving version on 26 September 1912, but finally abandoned it in 1914 as what he once condemned as a 'pure Dickens imitation'. In this American novel, with which he moved even further west than Paris, Kafka futuristically depicts the paradoxes that lie at the heart of the land of liberty, where justice means injustice, freedom entails enslavement to work, and progress leads back to the biblical curse of original sin. By 1914, however, the line that led from *The Judgement* had too powerfully 'driven' Kafka into new directions, involving a darker, more mysterious analysis. Only the first chapter, 'The Stoker', was published in his lifetime. This, his second book, appeared in 1913 under Kurt Wolff's new imprint, *The Day of Judgement*.

In the midst of his problems with *The Lost One*, on 17 November 1912, his first great inspiration continued to advance by progressive bifurcation, and he began *The Metamorphosis*, 'which came to me this morning in my misery in bed'. A week later, the tale is 'a little more than half finished', but then has to be set aside for a business trip: 'I'm so sorry about this, even if I hope the consequences are not too dire for the story, for which I still need 3–4 evenings.' Kafka believed that 'a story like this should be written with a maximum of one interruption in twice ten

'From a General Meeting of your Authors', a postcard to Kurt Wolff, 24 March 1913, signed by Kafka, Otto Pick, Albert Ehrenstein, Carl Ehrenstein, Paul Zech, and (on the reverse) Else Lasker-Schüler. Kafka's message relates to Werfel's having told Wolff about *The Metamorphosis*: 'Dear Mr. Wolff, don't believe Werfel! He doesn't know a word of my story. As soon as I have had a fair copy produced, I will of course be very glad to send it.'

The Metamorphosis, first edition, November 1915. Cover picture by Ottomar Starke. To prevent Starke attempting to draw Gregor Samsa, Kafka wrote to Wolff (25 October 1915): 'No, please don't! ... The insect itself cannot be drawn. It cannot even be shown from a distance.' Instead, Starke based his drawing on the father's reaction to Gregor's transformation.

hours'. Then it would possess natural 'drive'. On 3 December, he is 'just before the end', but cannot 'last through the night'. On the night of 5–6 December, he tells Felice Bauer, who is now his confidante: 'Cry, my beloved, cry, now is the time to cry! The hero of my little story died a little while ago.' The next night, it is all over: 'Dearest, so listen, my little story is finished, only I don't like today's conclusion, it could have been better, there's no doubt about it.'

The organic method Kafka willed into being corresponds to the textual coherence he desired, in which personal, social and existential themes enter a perfect fusion. From the opening sentence that announces Gregor Samsa's transformation into a giant insect, *The Metamorphosis* advances inexorably to his death. Gregor himself is an entomological wonder, a grotesque inversion of insect metamorphosis, in which a pent-up psychological truth manifests itself in a new, outer body – the only kind of beetle without any wings. As a living paradox, he exemplifies the story's organizing metaphor, 'a spineless creature'. Magically, the story adopts the victim's perspective, which produces both brief comic moments and a lasting pathos. Gregor's home is a model of capitalism, even to the extent that family rela-

Hotel Erzherzog Stephan (now Hotel Europa), Wenceslas Square (Wenzelsplatz/Václavské náměstí), where Kafka, appearing after Brod, Baum, Werfel, and Otto Pick, read *The Judgement* on 4 December 1912. He confessed to Felice afterwards: '... I have a hellish love of screaming into the ears of a well-prepared, attentive audience ...'

tions, ostensibly based on love, prove to be grounded in power, work, money, and exploitation. Gregor himself is finally swept aside by the maid as a mere 'dung beetle' – not unlike the 'enemies of the people' whose deaths Lenin justified by comparing them to 'noxious insects'. Thus Kafka revisits the motif of metamorphosis, the domain of myth, and, by finding it a home in a *petit bourgeois* family, demonstrates not the power of the gods, but the danger that underlies all existence.

Kafka planned to publish *The Judgement*, *The Stoker*, and *The Metamorphosis* in a volume called *The Sons* with Kurt Wolff, but this never happened, and Wolff brought out *The Metamorphosis* as a volume in 1915, followed by *The Judgement* in 1916. Kafka had successfully effected the transition from apprentice to major writer, whose work was in demand by one of the finest publishers of the day, and appeared alongside that of other major authors, like the poet, Georg Trakl. Yet fame was not his concern. Wolff observed that he never dealt with a writer so little interested in publication.

Kafka with Felice Bauer in 1917.

The Great War

My thoughts about the war, which eat me up in such very different
directions, are like the old anxieties about Felice ...

Kafka, *Diaries*

On 15 August 1912, when Kafka visited Max Brod at home to
finalize the contents of *Meditation*, he met Felice Bauer, to
whom he later dedicated *The Judgement*. Thus began his
longest and most tortured relationship, documented in over
500 letters and postcards that he sent her, sometimes as
often as two or three times a day, until late 1917. Just as he
transmuted his life into writing, he scriptualized Felice,
demanding from their union the same absolutes that he
imposed on his body, his ethics and his art. He did not just
'love' but 'worshipped' her, and expected her to provide his
'salvation'. He also demanded that his own words be 'true
and clear', so that he could '*somehow communicate to you the
beating of my heart*'. From the start, it was a tragic constella-
tion, in that she both mirrored and conflicted with his life
and needs. In family and social terms, it was a good match.
Yet for the writer, it spelled disaster. The daughter of an
insurance agent, Felice came from a family of assimilated
Berlin Jews, had a successful career as a manager in a hi-tech

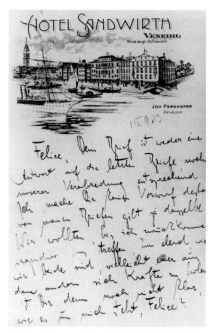

firm selling dictating machines and parlographs, and – to complete her westernizing credentials – even had a name that was pronounced in the French way. Notwithstanding her 'bony, empty face', her 'almost broken nose', her 'stiff, unattractive hair', when he first sat beside her, he formed an 'unshakeable judgement'. They talked, and she agreed to visit Palestine with him. In her person, he admired her resoluteness, her kindness and her liveliness. Yet their tastes differed. She wanted to fill their home with the ornate furniture that he hated, whereas he preferred modern simplicity. Worse still, she did not share his inter-

Kafka's letter to Felice Bauer from Venice, postmarked 16 September 1913: 'Felice, your letter is neither a reply to my last letters, nor does it accord to our agreement ... Do you still not realize, Felice, how things stand with me?' Apart from a card from Verona, this was his last letter to her for three months.

est in literature, and had little understanding for his art. Besides, he did not find her physically attractive, and she even brought out his feelings of sexual inadequacy. Yet he loved her passionately, such that his thoughts about her merged with his work. And so, at the very time when the duality between the office and his writing might have found a balance, he was beset by complications: 'I cannot live with her,' he told himself, 'and I cannot live without her.' The result was a psychological struggle, in which he internalized

the role of the lover bat-
tling against external
obstacles: 'I cannot believe
that a greater or more desperate battle for a woman
was ever waged in a fairy-
tale than was fought in me
over you, since the beginning, always anew, and
perhaps forever.'

In summer 1913, he for-
mulated the arguments for
and against marriage in his
diary, and by late that year,
relations had cooled. Then,
when Felice retreated,
Kafka, enlisting their inter-
mediary, Grete Bloch, now
pressed for marriage, and
on 1 June 1914 they
became officially engaged.

Franz Kafka aged about thirty.

However, Kafka experi-
enced the event at Felice's family apartment in Berlin as a
'torture', feeling 'bound like a criminal. If I had really been
bound in chains and had been set in the corner and had had
policemen placed before me and had been made to watch, it
could not have been worse'. Then, on 12 July – fourteen days
after the Archduke Ferdinand had been assassinated in Sara-
jevo – the engagement was dissolved at an acrimonious
meeting in Hôtel Askanischer Hof, Berlin, which, once again
resorting to legal terms, Kafka experienced as a 'court of justice'. His diary records:

The trip in the cab. F.'s face. She runs her fingers through her hair,

Hôtel Askanischer Hof, Berlin, the 'court of law' where Kafka's first engagement to Felice was annulled on 12 July 1914. The hotel stood near the Anhalter Bahnhof, and was frequented by many celebrities.

wipes her nose, yawns. Suddenly she pulls herself together and says something well prepared, hostile things she had long been saving up.

The trip back with Miss Bloch. The room in the hotel, the heat reflected from the wall opposite. Heat also from the vaulted walls which enclose the window. In addition, the afternoon sun. The nimble waiter, almost eastern Jewish. Noise in the courtyard, as if from an engineering works. Bad smells. The bedbug. Hard decision to squash it. Chambermaid astonished: there are no bugs anywhere, only once a guest found one in the corridor. At her parents'. Her mother's occasional single tears. I recite my lesson. Her father understands the matter correctly from every angle. Came from Malmö just for my sake, travelled all night, sits there in shirt-sleeves. They agree with me, there is nothing or not much that can be said against me. Devilish in all my innocence. Apparent guilt of Miss Bloch. In the evening alone on a seat in Unter den Linden.

Hotel Schloss Balmoral und Osborne in Marien bad, where Kafka and Felice stayed in July 1916. 'I was intimate with Felice only in letters, humanly I have only been so for two days. It is not so clear. Doubts remain. But the look from her soothing eyes is beautiful, the opening of her feminine depths ...' (6 July 1916).

Riva, Lake Garda, which Kafka visited in September–October 1913, the scene of his romance with an eighteen-year-old 'Swiss girl'. The harbour at Riva is the setting for *The Hunter Gracchus*, in which the hero is both 'dead', and, 'to some extent ... also alive ...'

The capitulation was followed by another reversal. They met again in 1915, and in July 1916 spent ten days together in adjoining rooms with a communicating door at a hotel in Marienbad. Kafka wrote to Brod of:

> ... a series of terrible days stirred up by even more terrible nights. It really seemed to me that the rat had reached its final hole. But as it couldn't get any worse, it got better. The cords with which I am bound were at least loosened, I set myself to rights, and she, who had always thrust her hands out to help me into the complete emptiness, helped again and I entered a completely unknown relationship with her, from one human being to another, which approached the one which in our best times I had had as a letter writer to her as the recipient of my letters. I was never really intimate

Kafka

with a woman before, except twice, that time in Zuckmantel [Zlaté Hory] (but there she was a woman and I was a boy) and the one in Riva (but there she was half a child and I was completely confused and sick in every direction under the sun). But now I saw a woman's trusting look and could not shut myself off. Some things have been torn open that I will always wish to preserve (not single things, but a whole) and out of this opening, I know, enough unhappiness will come for more than one lifetime ...

Kafka with Ottla, his 'best friend', at the entrance to the Oppelt House, 6 (now 5) Old Town Square, where he lived from November 1913 – Summer 1914. Note the bandage on his thumb that he was 'curing by natural means'.

Kafka and Felice now became engaged for a second time and planned to marry after the war. However, when the inner 'wound' manifested itself as tuberculosis later that year, this second engagement was also aborted. The two earlier occasions on which he had been 'intimate' with a woman – on holiday in 1905, and in Riva in 1913 when he had enjoyed an innocent romance with a young Swiss girl – only emphasized his anguished solitude.

The first time that Kafka and Felice broke, the episode at the 'court room' thrust him into despair. On returning home, he noted: 'My inability to think, to observe, to ascertain, to remember, to speak, to experience is becoming ever greater, I am turning to stone ... ' And then: 'If I don't rescue myself in

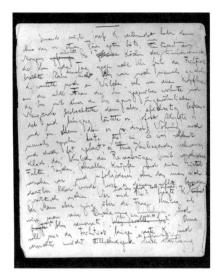

The first page of the manuscript of *The Trial*.

Soldiers in Prague in the First World War.

a piece of work, I am lost.' Next day, on 29 July 1914, he began a fragment, continuing a long string of abandoned beginnings that seems to anticipate *The Trial*. Here he draws out the implications inherent in the legal language he had from the very start used to describe his relationship with Felice (present in the novel as Fräulein Bürstner), in order to pass 'judgement' on his life – and on the world. His personal dilemma had begun to mirror a universal crisis, as the diaries make clear by tacitly juxtaposing his own difficulties with the political arena. Taking back *The Trial* even before he had properly started, he comments: 'Begun failed works. But I won't give up, in spite of my sleeplessness, headaches, general incapacity. It is the last life force that has gathered for this purpose.' Two days later, war is imminent: 'I have no time. General mobilization ... Now I will receive the reward of my solitude. But it's hardly a reward. Solitude brings punishments. Still, I'm hardly touched by the misery, and more decided than ever.' Then, on the fateful day, 2 August 1914: 'Germany has declared war on Russia. – Afternoon to the swimming school.' The longstanding inner struggle that Kafka maintained between east and west is now overtaken by political reality, from which he seeks momentary refuge in an absurd denial. By 6 August, when he has watched the artillery pass through Prague, the pose breaks down: 'I am shattered,' he comments. 'Full of lies, hatred, and envy. Full of incapacity, stupidity, dull-wittedness. Full of laziness, weakness, and defencelessness. 31 years old ... ' The parallelism between his own crisis and the negativity of the world is subsumed by his universal horror. Indeed, at a time when even leading German-speaking writers like Rilke and Mann were carried away by war fever, and only a handful, notably Karl Kraus, actually attacked the war, Kafka stands apart, totalizing the world's negativity in his own, remorseless self-criticism, and taking upon himself the burden of guilt. Just as he had originally

Karel Šviha, a Czech Member of Parliament, was accused of being an Austrian spy by a Czech newspaper in March 1913 but, after a scandal lasting about a year, failed to clear his name in court in May 1914, just a few months before Kafka began *The Trial*. The novel echoes various aspects of the Šviha affair, in which a single dubious accusation led to a man's destruction.

conceived *The Judgement* as a story about a war, the First World War provided a context for his novel. He worked on *The Trial* from August 1914, making good progress until early October, but then slowed down, and his diary voices increasing complaints about poor progress, until he abandoned the novel on 20 January 1915: 'End of writing. When will it take me up again?' There is hardly an echo of the war in the book. True, there is something military about the uniforms that the men wear who arrest Joseph K., with their 'various pleats, pockets, buckles, buttons, and a belt', and their names, too – Franz and Willem – playfully recall the German and Austrian Emperors who led Europe into the abyss, Kaiser Franz Josef and Kaiser Wilhelm. Yet if the war provides the novel's historical context, by the end of 1914 Kafka had siphoned off the theme into the only completed text from this period, *In the Penal Colony*, which, with its terrible killing machine, symbolizes the battle between two world orders, an archaic, absolute law, and a supposedly humane, liberal society. That left the way clear for *The Trial* to explore quite different concerns.

From the first, western setting of *The Lost One*, Kafka's novels move eastwards to his home-town in *The Trial*, and even further east with the snowbound village landscape of *The Castle* – a spiritual geography alluded to ironically in the name of the castle's owner, Count Westwest. The terrible power that his art unleashes in *The Trial*, with its barely hinted parallels between inner crisis and political cataclysm, also reflects a growing preoccupation with Russian literature, and specifically with Dostoyevsky, who, along with Kleist and Flaubert, Kafka counted as one of his genuine 'blood relatives'. *Crime and Punishment* provides a frame for Kafka's own metaphysical thriller, into which, however, Kafka injects the lurid scenery of the Prague *fin-de-siècle* also deployed in Gustav Meyrink's novel, *The Golem*, which had been serialized in 1913–14.

It is Kafka's blackest novel. Expanding on his experiences with his father, Felice, his town, and his job, *The Trial* turns the law into an obscure metaphor of the world order, while Joseph K.'s battle with authority, evoking an allegory for the human condition, expands into a crusade for justice and a quest for truth. The Court, which should uphold justice, is vindictive, corrupt, and cruel. The law is invisible, yet invincible. Charges are never laid; defence is banned; bureaucracy is all-enveloping; the judges unknown, ranked in a near infinite hierarchy; and the

František Drtikol: *The Courtyards of Prague, No. 11* (1911). The typically sombre atmosphere of early Prague modernism captured by Drtikol, Meyrink and others reappears in *The Trial*.

accused is a victim, whose guilt is inescapable, and whose death is inevitable. The nature, meaning, and function of the law all remain mysterious: it is a labyrinth from which there is no escape. Indeed, the law may even be imaginary. There is no certainty. Yet, as a supreme authority, it paradoxically embodies justice, truth, knowledge and power, while its operations combine the methods of a total State with almost supernatural forces. And secularizing the Hebrew prayer 'The Lord shall bless thy coming in and thy going out', it even assumes metaphysical proportions: 'The Court asks nothing of you. It admits you when you come, and releases you when

Josef Sudek (1896–1976): from the series *St Vitus's Cathedral* (1924–8). Prague's oldest, most splendid church, begun in 1344 by Matthias von Arras and continued by Peter Parler and his sons, photographed by the leading Czech photographer. The setting for the cathedral scene in *The Trial*.

you go.' Thus, via *The Trial*, Kafka accomplishes an extraordinary leap into spirituality, as near the end he rewrites ancient lore: in the scene imagined in Prague's Saint Vitus's cathedral, the Priest recounts a religious parable, *Before the Law*. By interpreting it, K. reaches the bitter truth underlying the modern situation, that 'the Lie' has been elevated to 'the world order'. Hence, the novel counters the world's darkness by asserting moral values, and raising the faint prospect of illumination. Kafka read the parable to Felice early in 1915, and other parts, too, to Brod, who remarked in his diary: 'He is the greatest writer of our day.'

Kafka uncannily divides himself into both narrator and anti-hero, accuser and accused. This method lies behind the figure in whom we may recognize a new Everyman. Within a contemporary framework provided by Mach's critique of the 'subject', his closely focused grasp of perspectival limitation, and his view that physical and mental reality are equal, Kafka develops a fictional figure, 'K.', whose psychology anticipates Freud's later triad – id, ego, super-ego – and who acts according to unpredictable drives and compulsions; but no less importantly the portrayal of K. also contains features later defined in gestalt psychology, which regards the self as a holistic system, interacting with the environment, and operating according to mechanical and dynamic laws. Beneath these contemporary strata, the depiction of Joseph K.'s mind exhibits much older attributes. Presenting his behaviour in such a way as to invite praise or blame belongs to what Locke calls 'forensic' psychology. K.'s actual emotions often resemble the medieval deadly sins, notably pride, anger, lust, sloth, and avarice (he works in a bank), and he seeks out a single cardinal virtue, justice, which the novel juxtaposes with a single, fundamental category, namely 'guilt'. However, the translucent style fuses these different strata into a single whole, both a modern, scientific 'psyche', and a traditional, religious 'soul'.

Insofar as *The Trial* and *The Castle* reflect Austria–Hungary, like Hašek's *Švejk* and Musil's *The Man without Qualities*, Kafka's novels reflect a bureaucratic, hierarchical and bungling, but deadly, Empire. However, Kafka himself was

Adolphe Roehn: *Bivouac de Napoléon sur le champ de bataille de Wagram nuit de 5–6 juillet 1809*. Kafka was fascinated by Napoleon, describing this picture in his Paris diary (1911), and often identifying with him in later life.

also intrigued by other exponents of power like Alexander and Napoleon, the charismatic world conqueror. In Versailles, he was particularly struck by Adolphe Roehn's painting of Napoleon, and at home, he would have been familiar with the legend that Napoleon had visited Prague and stopped by in the hostelry u Šnelů, which took its name (the German *schnell*) from Napoleon's order 'Vitesse, vitesse, vitesse!' In his letters to Felice, he uses a coded reference to the findings at Napoleon's post mortem to explain his own sexual inadequacies, and during the war, his diaries evince considerable interest in Napoleon's Russian campaign. What fascinates him about Napoleon's 'error' in invading Russia is the dual paradox that his aim was impossible, yet from the start he will have known what to expect: this pattern also emerges in *The Trial*, and is fundamental to *The Castle* and some of the later stories. The 'conquering' streak that he recognized in his father's family clearly had a place in Kafka's own make-up, albeit contradicted by the certainty of failure, and was channelled into a literary campaign, where, in breaking new ground, Kafka's writing acted out the military metaphor of the 'avant-garde'. He adopts this pose when speaking of his art as a form of 'military service', and terms his writing habits as being 'on manoeuvre' (returning home after the office, sleeping in the afternoon, and writing at night).

Though numerous Prague intellectuals were conscripted, for different reasons, Kafka's circle remained intact. He had to present himself for inspection three times between 1915 and 1917, but although found fit to serve, the office – much to his annoyance – would not release him. As he records: 'The next task is unconditional: to become a soldier.' His motives are hard to probe. He did not support the war, and though conscription might superficially have resolved his personal problems, more fundamentally the plan manifests a sense of responsibility, as well as the Kafkas' propensity to 'conquer'. Moreover, military service would have completed his 'immersion' in the negativity of the age, which he witnessed during his own fruitless efforts on behalf of shell-shocked soldiers, the 'victims of endless, constantly increasing suffering', who had now become mere 'candidates for the lunatic asylum'.

The Final Rupture

It was like this. The brain could no longer bear the worries and pains that were imposed on it. It said: 'I'm giving up; but if there is anyone else here who is interested in preserving the whole, let him assume part of my burden and it will be alright for a bit.' Then the lung spoke up ...

To Milena

The house at Bilekgasse 10 (Bílkova ulice), where Kafka spent the first few weeks of the war and started writing *The Trial*.

At the outbreak of war, Kafka resumed his peripatetic existence. In October–November 1913, the family had moved to a new home, a six-roomed apartment on the third floor of the Oppelt House at 6 Old Town Square (now No. 5), but, in August 1914, Kafka transferred to Valli's apartment at 10 Bilekgasse (Bílkova ulice), where he started *The Trial*. Then, from September 1914, he moved to her house at 46 Nerudova in Vinohrady,

Painting of Nerudova (1907) by Jindřich Tomec (1863–1928), the well-known Czech painter who lived mainly in Vienna. Nerudova is the main thoroughfare, lined with little shops and inns, which leads through the Lesser Town (Kleinseite/Malá Strana) to the Castle. Kafka would normally have used this route on his way to Golden Lane.

but in February returned to Bilekgasse as a lodger for just over a month. After that, he settled at 18 (now No. 16) Langegasse (Dlouhá) from March 1915 until February 1917. While living at Langegasse, he and Ottla went in search of a suitable place for him to write, and alighted on the little house in the Prague Castle at 22 Golden Lane (Alchimistengasse/Zlatá

A drawing from Kafka's octavo notebook from the time he rented a room in Golden Lane. The hill recalls the steep roads leading up to the Prague Castle.

The little house at 22 Golden Lane (now painted dark grey), which Ottla rented for Kafka in 1916–17. As he told Felice, 'it was like the fulfilment of a dream ...'

The old steps leading from the Prague Castle. After writing in Golden Lane, Kafka enjoyed walking down here 'towards midnight'.

ulička), which had once housed Rudolf II's alchemists. Here, from late autumn 1916, he worked at night and then walked home 'down the castle steps to the old town'. The stories he now produced drew out the aesthetic sum of *The Trial*: the dream-like *A Country Doctor*, which probably originated in February 1917, brings the problem of guilt to a head in the description of a young boy's 'enormous wound', but in other tales, the theme recedes, and the new, symbolic style of *Before the Law* leads to short texts like *The Bucket Rider* written in January – which recalls Kubin's cyclist, lost in the void – and the parable *An Imperial Message*, datable to mid-March, as well as *On the Gallery*, which marks the turn to tales about performing artistes. Then, in March, he rented two rooms in the splendid Schön-born Palais in the Lesser Town (Kleinseite/Malá Strana), where *A Report for an Academy* was written. However, about six month after diagnosing his fictional child's 'incurable' complaint in *A Country Doctor*, he fell ill himself, coughing up blood in the night of 12–13 August 1917, and so went back to the family again in the Oppelt House, living in Ottla's room, which he retained until June 1920.

To an unusual extent, Kafka remained embedded in what he once called the 'family animal', and family experiences of all kinds pervade his work. As a student, he holidayed with his Uncle Siegfried Löwy, whom he remembers in *A Country Doctor*, and other family members also fuelled his imagina-tion. Two maternal uncles, Joseph and Alfred Löwy, visited America, and provided Kafka with details that entered *The Lost One*, while the hero's 'crime' – he is seduced by the cook – actually occurred to his cousin, Robert Kafka, whose American career is in some ways reflected in the book. Then there was Uncle Joseph Löwy's earlier life in the Belgian Congo, where he worked building a railway: impressions from the tropics filtered into *In the Penal Colony*, while his occupation reappears in the unfinished *Memories of the Kalda Railway* that Kafka wrote while working on *The Trial*, and which exchanges the exotic Congolese setting for the Russian steppes. Later, when Kafka fell ill, he turned to his sister Ottla.

Kafka did not believe the doctors' euphemistic diagnosis of his pulmonary tuberculosis, but still reacted with equa-nimity. If, as Susan Sontag argues, illness is a metaphor,

Franz Kafka's uncle, Siegfried Löwy (1867–1942), photographed in 1914. One of the four girls pushing his motorcycle is Ottla (far left). Writing to Brod from his holidays with his uncle in 1907, Kafka notes: 'I am riding a lot on a motor-bike ...'

then tuberculosis was a metaphor both for artistic sensibility and for the modernist crisis, which is how Thomas Mann employs it in *The Magic Mountain* to diagnose the political tensions that culminated in the First World War. Kafka preferred to interpret it in terms of his own self. On 15 September 1917, shortly after his 'wound' had become apparent, he decided that it offered him an opportunity:

You have the chance to make a fresh start, insofar as the possibility exists at all. Don't waste it. If you want to force your way inside, you won't avoid the dirt that wells up. But don't wallow in it. If the wound in your lung is only a symbol, as you claim, a symbol of the

wound, an infection called F., and whose depth is called justification, if this is really the case, then the medical advice (light, air, sun, rest) is a symbol. Take hold of the symbol.

With this insight, and in his increasingly desperate state, his writing entered its next phase, in which he aimed 'to elevate life into the pure, the true, and the unchanging'. He used his first sick leave from September 1917 until April 1918 to visit Ottla in the country at Zürau (Siřem), living with her in a 'small, good marriage'. Besides his physical suffering, the involvement with Felice haunted him still, until, after she visited him, he finally broke with her at Christmas 1917. To his evident relief, she soon got married. In this time of crisis, he turned once

Left Elli aged twenty-one. This picture, like that of Valli, was probably taken as part of a series intended to enhance the children's marriage prospects. Elli married in 1910, Valli in 1913 and Ottla in 1920. This all increased the pressure on Kafka to find a wife.

Right Valli aged 20. Kafka's affection for his sisters extended to their children, and Elli's daughter Gerti recalls his profound influence on them all, notably by introducing them to 'everything precious and beautiful and also to everything that was difficult and inexplicable'.

more to Kierkegaard – he had noted an affinity in 1913 – and in early 1918 read *Either/Or* and *Fear and Trembling*, which helped him to reground his writing yet again.

He had recently written some reflective texts, and now developed this mode. His aphorisms of 1917–18 refine and redefine his vision. Kafka collected them into a manuscript, which Brod, recognizing their importance, published as *Reflections on Sin, Suffering, Hope, and the True Way*. These short texts confront widely differing traditions, notably Judaism, Christianity, Platonism, the Tao, Existentialism, Psychoanalysis, and Relativity Theory. Kafka's fascination with circus artistry returns in his re-working of the Nietzschean acrobat image: 'I err. The true way leads over a tight-rope which is not placed high up, but just above the ground. It seems to be designed to make you stumble rather than to be walked across.' The Taoist 'Way' turns into an absurdly practical problem.

Many aphorisms revolve around one image, expressing a complex argument in vivid, poetic form: 'To grasp the good fortune that the ground upon which you stand can be no larger than the two feet which cover it.' The text gains resonance when read against the topical insistence – German, Czech, Zionist – on a national 'ground'. Countering any kind of 'homeland', Kafka – still arguing dialectically with Bergman, twenty years on! – asserts a humility, and renegotiates the mind–body problem by means of mental acrobatics: we must internalize his idea by thinking from head to toe. A powerful identity emerges between acting, writing, thinking, and being, as the self divests itself of baggage: 'Believing means: to liberate the indestructible in oneself or more correctly: to liberate oneself or

Kafka with Ottla at the entrance to their home in Zürau (Siřem), north-western Bohemia (1917–18). From 1913, Kafka worked part-time as a gardener, and, inspired by his example, Ottla also turned to agriculture. After the diagnosis of his illness, he attempted a cure by going to stay in the country with her.

A view of Zürau (Siřem), sent by Kafka and Ottla to Max Brod (20 September 1917). Although Kafka wrote no major stories here, the experience contributed to the depiction of village life in *The Castle*.

more correctly: being indestructible or more correctly: being.'

Writing is a quest for existence, in which Kafka confronts the world with a metaphysical order, as in the following utterance, that treats a close relative of the jackdaw or *kavka*, the crow: 'The crows maintain: a single crow could destroy the sky. That is certainly true, but it is no proof against the sky, because the sky means: the impossibility of crows.' The absolute, a 'sky' or 'heaven' (the German *Himmel* means both), remains in suspended contradiction with its inhabitants, the 'crows'.

Sin, pain, suffering, truth, ethics, and religion are fundamental to these aphorisms. Man's task resides in 'negativity', since he already possesses the 'positive'; and the real world is pure 'spirit': 'It is not actually the material world that is unreal, but the evil within it which in our eyes constitutes the world of the senses.'

Kafka produced another collection of aphorisms in 1920, called *He*, which, like the earlier ones, merge with his fiction. Some aphorisms are actually miniature stories, and are closely connected to the burst of parables, fables, and anecdotes that flowed forth in 1917–23, such as *A Commentary* (entitled *Give it up!* by Brod):

It was very early in the morning, the streets were clean and empty, I was going to the station. When I compared my watch with the tower clock, I saw that it was already much later than I had thought. I had to hurry. The shock at the discovery made me uncertain about my way. I did not know my way around the town very well. Fortunately there was a policeman nearby. I ran to him and breathlessly asked him the way. He smiled and said: 'You want to know the way from me?' 'Yes,' I said, 'since I cannot find it myself.' 'Give up, give up,' he said, and turned away with a grand gesture, like someone who wishes to be alone with his laughter.

The anecdote revolves around an episode, which, like many of Kafka's best works, involves a metaphysical accident on the borders between space, time, and the mind. The world goes awry, authority collapses, communication ceases, and absurdity reigns supreme.

In later years, Kafka turned increasingly towards Judaism, but the relationship was never simple. His closest friends – Bergman, Brod, Weltsch – were leading members of the Prague Zionist circle, which was strongly influenced by Martin Buber. Kafka met Buber in 1913, visited him with Felice on their engagement day, and published *A Report for an Academy* in Buber's journal, *Der Jude*, in 1917. Kafka also evinced an interest in Zionism, and towards the end of his life considered emigrating to Palestine. But the plan, as he indicated to Milena in 1920, did not imply belief. Just like Schönberg, when he broke with Kandinsky on account of the latter's anti-semitism, Kafka recognized the future because it was all around him:

I now spend every afternoon in the streets and bathe in anti-semitism, and I once now heard the Jews called a 'prašivé plemeno' [i.e. dirty breed]. Isn't it obvious that one should leave a place where one is hated (Zionism or national feeling are not necessary for that)? The heroism that consists in staying behind is that of the cockroaches, that cannot be exterminated in the bathroom.

I have just looked out of the window: mounted police, gendarmes ready for a bayonet charge on the crowd, and up here the disgusting dishonour of always having to live under protection.

The conclusion of hostilities in 1918 and the declaration of the Czechoslovak Republic in October that year, with its violent sentiment against Austria, did nothing to alleviate the political tensions experienced by Prague's German-speaking Jews.

The Last Earthly Frontier

Just a word. Just a request. Just a movement of the air. Just a proof
that you are still alive and waiting. No, not a request, just breath,
not breath just readiness, not readiness just a thought, not a
thought just peaceful sleep.

Kafka, *Fragments*

Kafka's literary career, if modest, was not without success. In
1915, when Carl Sternheim was awarded the Fontane Prize, it
was at Blei's recommendation that he passed the money on
to Kafka. This publicity stunt was duly exploited by Kafka's
publisher. Blei's early insight into Kafka's 'negative capability'
(he uses Keats's term), and his assertion that Kafka was the
'servant of a God in whom he did not believe', indicates the
extent to which not just local writers but also his Viennese
contemporaries took him seriously. Indeed, when Karl Kraus
wanted to satirize the prodigality of the Prague German writers, he did so in an untranslatable Schiller parody that pun-
ningly connects the names of Werfel, Brod, Kafka, and Kisch
to suggest a bubbling spring (*'Es brodelt und werfelt und
kafkat und kischt'*). Another key Viennese figure to recognize
Kafka was Robert Musil, who in 1914 tried to enlist him for
Die Neue Rundschau, but the planned publication of *The
Metamorphosis* was prevented by the editor, and Musil had to

content himself with reviewing *The Stoker* – a notice Kafka much appreciated – and visiting him in Prague.

Kafka's presence as a writer in Germany was guaranteed by Kurt Wolff, who established himself as the most significant publishing figure of the Expressionist generation, and when Kafka thought of breaking with him, there were other publishers waiting in the wings. *In the Penal Colony* caused some problems; Kafka considered publishing it with *The Judgement* and *The Metamorphosis* in a collection called *Punishments*. After haverings on both sides, Wolff eventually brought it out as a single volume in 1919, and that year also published *A Country Doctor*, a collection of thirteen new stories. However, he ran into financial difficulties, and when Kafka finally decided to live as a writer, he changed publisher, and it was Die Schmiede in Berlin that brought out his final collection of four stories, *A Hunger Artist*, in August 1924.

Although he knew many writers in Prague, Vienna, and Berlin, Kafka cultivated a relatively small number of friends. Among the Prague writers it was chiefly the Expressionist poet Franz Werfel – who married Alma Mahler, Gustav Mahler's widow – whose company he enjoyed. Once, he notes being 'smashed and elevated' by Werfel's pathos-

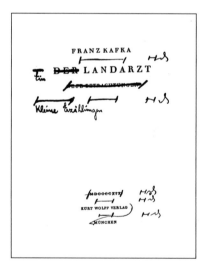

Kafka's proof corrections to the title page of *A Country Doctor*.

Opposite The first edition of Kafka's *In the Penal Colony* (1919).

FRANZ KAFKA

IN DER
STRAFKOLONIE

ERZÄHLUNG

Kafka and his friend, the writer Ernst Weiss (1882–1940), holidaying by the sea at Marielyst, Denmark (1914). Weiss, a doctor by training, had turned to literature to save himself from tuberculosis. He supported Kafka's decision not to marry, assisted him in his problems with Felice, witnessed the annulment in Berlin, and then took him to the sea. 'A very kind, very trustworthy, in certain respects – but only in certain respects – highly insightful and in happy moments a splendidly lively person' (Kafka to Felice, 18 May 1914).

driven poems. Another time, Werfel left in tears after Kafka's silent criticism. Ernst Weiss, like Kafka another 'western Jew', briefly acted as a kind of double, helping him during his difficulties with Felice. But the intimacy did not last, and Brod remained his closest friend. It was Brod who became the first reader of *The Castle*, Brod whom Kafka made his literary executor, and Brod's astute publishing of the posthumous novels and over thirty stories as well as other writings and fragments – against Kafka's instructions to burn them all – that ensured Kafka's lasting fame.

With success, Kafka became more private, more intent on finding a home, more orientated on a distant east. His 'east' had a complex, stratified geography. It began in Prague. The name Austria in German (Österreich) means 'eastern kingdom', and so Kafka's home town could already be regarded as lying in the east. From there, it extended to the Bohemian countryside, where the village Jews lived, and further on via Moravia and Slovakia to Galicia, whence hundreds of Jewish refugees had flooded into Prague during the war, and over to the Ukraine of the Hassidim. Then again, Kafka's east also encompassed Dostoyevsky's Russia, with its rivers, steppes, and snowy wastes. Further still, it included China. The nineteenth century had already compared the rambling Austro-Hungarian Empire to China, and signs of the 'middle kingdom' could also be found in Prague, in the shape of the Hunger Wall, which provided an inspiration for Kafka's *Great Wall*

Sixteenth-century engraving of Prague showing the Hunger Wall (Hungermauer/Hladová Zed˘), Charles Bridge (still without its sculptures) and the Old Town. The wall reappears in Kafka's *Great Wall of China*.

of China. Writing once to Felice, Kafka, ever fascinated by China, called himself 'essentially Chinese' – the very term incidentally Ernst Weiss used for Mozart, because of his simple 'spirituality'. The conflict between west and east also involved the distinction – derived from Tönnies' typology – between a western, capitalist 'society' and an organic 'community', whether in Palestine or China. Hence Kafka could link Judaism, China and the simple life, or comment to Brod that 'gardening and Hebrew' were his two chief achievements. These thoughts issue in Kafka's fables, whose animals share the traits of very different peoples, as well as in his third novel, with its quest for a home among a peasant community in a rural, snowy landscape, overseen by a rambling, bureaucratic castle.

When illness struck, the need for a home became urgent. Sickness itself had long been the determining opposite of Kafka's desire for health. Nervousness, sleeplessness and headaches were frequent complaints. He writes to Brod that his headaches resemble the feeling in a pane of glass 'at the moment when it cracks'. He explains: 'For some time, I have been complaining of an illness, but never have a particular illness.' At around this time, the Viennese doctor, J. B. Andreatti, recognized that such states were typical of

Pension Stüdl at Schelesen (Želízy), where Kafka stayed in 1918–19. The balcony in the foreground belonged to his room, in which he wrote *Letter to My Father*.

incipient tuberculosis. In Kafka's case, as in so many others, this remained undiagnosed; when it was recognized, although the condition was still curable, it was too late. Various factors exacerbated the disease: the insurance company's refusal to pension him off, making him accept leave, often briefer than recommended; his attempt to recover by living in the country, avoiding the sanatoria, which, in his early years, had promoted his health, but now involved sickness; and his spiritual acceptance of death: 'From a certain point, there is no going back. That is the point to reach.'

Julie Wohryzek (1891–1944), Kafka's second fiancée. Writing to Brod, he describes her as 'in love with films, operettas and comedies, with powder and veils, possessed of an inexhaustible and unstoppable store of the cheekiest Yiddish expressions, altogether very ignorant, more cheerful than sad ...' (6 February 1919).

The benefits of the stay with Ottla were short-lived, and so he moved to a pension at Schelesen (Želízy) in late 1918. Here he met the 26-year-old Julie Wohryzek. Like Kafka himself, Julie was a Prague Jew who had come to Schelesen seeking a cure for tuberculosis. By summer 1919, when he was back at work in Prague, they were inseparable. His thoughts turned to marriage, and they were engaged in September. This time, however, it was Kafka's father who objected, remonstrating with him for taking 'just anyone' – Julie's family was

Milena Jesenská (1896–1944), the Czech journalist and translator, who approached Kafka for permission to translate his work in 1919–20, and with whom he had a passionate, tortured and ultimately doomed romance, chiefly by correspondence.

impoverished – and recommending a 'brothel' instead. Kafka and Julie continued with their wedding preparations, though, and only broke off the engagement when their plan to rent an apartment fell through. The failure, with Hermann Kafka's violent 'humiliation' of his son, provided the immediate impulse for *Letter to My Father*, which Kafka wrote, back again in Schelesen that November. With barely controlled anger, he launches a ferocious analysis, seeking to explore their entire relationship down to its roots in his infancy, not to apportion 'blame', but – pathetically – in an attempt to set things right. His whole life now seemed but one long struggle, in which: 'My writing was about you ...' If Kafka's later work displays a new sense of ease, an openness to reconciliation, perhaps the letter effected a catharsis. On Ottla's advice, he never sent it.

While Kafka and Julie were still meeting, he fell desperately in love with Milena Jesenská, a 25-year-old writer and journalist, who had approached him in the winter of 1919–20 about translating his work. Milena came from an old Czech family, had severe problems with her own authoritarian father, and shared Kafka's passion for literature. However, she was married to Ernst Pollak, and lived in Vienna. Once again, the relationship was doomed. Kafka called Milena 'a living fire such as I have never seen before', and soon she became his 'angel': 'Sensitive, brave, and bright, she throws everything into her sacrifice or, if you will, owes everything to sacrifice ...' They quickly became intimate in their letters, as Kafka explained: 'My world is collapsing, and my world is rebuilding itself.' He visited her in Vienna, and according to Milena he completely 'lost his anxiety' in her company, but, as she recalled, she was 'too weak to join him'. Her inability to leave

Merano, South Tyrol (northern Italy), where Kafka stayed in 1920, and from where he began his correspondence with Milena.

Drawing which Kafka sent to Milena, probably in September 1920. 'So that you can see something of my "occupations", I am enclosing a drawing. It shows four poles. Rods have been driven through the two central ones to which the "delinquent's" hands are fastened. Rods for the feet are passed through the two outer ones. After the man is bound, the rods are slowly drawn outwards, until the man is torn in half in the middle. The inventor is leaning on a pillar with crossed arms and legs. He looks very important, as if this were all his own invention, whereas he only copied the butcher's display of a disembowelled pig in front of his shop.'

her husband effectively put an end to the affair, although they met again in Gmünd (on the border between Austria and Czechoslovakia), and continued seeing each other. His confidence in her was almost limitless, as is indicated by his giving her the manuscripts of the *Letter to My Father*, *The Lost One*, and all his diaries, which end in June 1922. She seems to have understood him better than anyone, writing:

We all seem able to live because we have at one time or another taken refuge in a lie, in blindness, enthusiasm, or optimism, in a belief, in pessimism, or whatever. But he has never fled to a protective refuge, nowhere. He is absolutely incapable of lying, just as he is incapable of getting drunk. He has no refuge, no home. That is why he is exposed to everything from which we are protected. He is like a naked man ...

Kafka eventually visited a sanatorium in the Vienna Woods in October 1920, when it was discovered that both his lungs were affected, and in December he decided on a cure at Matliary in the High Tatra Mountains. Here, he met the young medical student, Robert Klopstock, who shared his passion for Dostoyevsky, and assumed the familiar role of Kafka's

'Villa Tatra', Matliary (High Tatras), where Kafka stayed in 1920–21: 'A good place, which has a semblance of being a sanatorium but is not ... it admits hunters and all and sundry ... and only makes you pay for what you actually eat ...' (31 December 1920). His first-floor room had the balcony to the left of the corner in the foreground.

Below Kafka with friends at Matliary, including the daughters of the owner, Alexander Bugsch. *Seated* (from the left): Margarete Bugsch, the dentist Dr Glauber, Susanne Golgen (rear), an unidentified woman (front), Kafka, Ilonka Roth. *Standing*: first and fourth: probably staff; second: Irene Bugsch; centre: the Hungarian medical student Robert Klopstock (1899–1972), who became a close friend and nursed Kafka in his final illness.

Spindelmühle (Špindlerův Mlýn) in the Giant
Mountains, where Kafka began *The Castle* in 1922.

double: 'I only relate to the
medical student,' he com-
mented to Brod, 'if some-
one wants something from me, they tell him.' Yet he rejected
the actual treatment: 'Tuberculosis no more has its seat in the
lungs than the World War had in the ultimatum. There is only
one disease ... ' He returned to Prague, more desolate than
ever – 'I can't even bear people's gaze ... ' – and his leave was
extended to early 1922, when he suffered a nervous 'collapse'.
In 'boundless despair' he formulated a 'nocturnal decision',
which led him further on what Erich Heller has called 'the
artist's journey into the interior'. Kafka records:
'If there is a transmigration of souls then I am not yet on the
bottom rung. My life is a hesitation before birth.' Wishing to
depart to 'another planet', he went back to the mountains,
now choosing Spindelmühle (Špindlerův Mlýn). Uncannily,
reality caught up with his inventions when the authorities
put him down as 'Joseph K.' His nocturnal decision may have
involved the resolution to produce a major work. He had
been unproductive for a while, and at Spindelmühle made

Friedrich Feigl: Sketch of Kafka reading *The Bucket Rider*, pen and ink (1946). Kafka liked Feigl's work and once commissioned a picture from him. The sketch, which recalls a private reading in Prague, is the only portrait of Kafka drawn by a close acquaintance.

notes that prefigure *The Castle*, remarking in his diary on: 'The strange, mysterious, perhaps dangerous, perhaps redemptive comfort of writing ... ' He reflects on the question of 'guilt'. He feels that he has entered 'another world'. A power called 'he' does not permit him to live 'in his world'. Then, finally, on 29 January, experience once again elides into fiction:

Assaults on the path in the snow in the evening. Ever the mixture of ideas, roughly like this: In this world the situation would be terrible, alone here in Sp., on top of that on a deserted path, on which you always slip in the snow in the darkness, on top of that it's a meaningless path without an earthly goal (to the bridge? Why there? In any case, I didn't even reach it), on top of that in a deserted village ... incapable of bearing a meeting with anyone ... I cannot love ... I am too far away ...

Kafka in Old Town Square before the Oppelt Haus around the time he was working on *The Castle* (1922).

Kafka, not unironically, imagines a leader figure,

both spiritual and military, linking Moses in the wilderness, Napoleon in Russia, and, more topically, explorers like Scott and Amundsen at the Pole in 1912:

The clearest thing of all is that I, being assaulted by powerful enemies on the right and on the left, can only go forwards, a hungry animal; the path leads to edible food, breathable air, a free life, and be it beyond life itself. You lead the masses, long, tall general, lead the despairing people through the pass that cannot be found by anyone else beneath the snow. And who gives you the power? The one who gives you the clarity of your vision.

More smoothly than ever, it seems, *in extremis*, Kafka's life transcends to art, and in the novel itself, all the recent anguish over Julie and Milena returns, transmuted, in fictive guise, where Julie perhaps assumes the imagined shape of Olga, the 'childish girl', Milena reappears as Frieda, and the chief obstacle to a union, her husband, becomes the grotesque Klamm, the castle official. From private suffering *The Castle* ascends into a metaphysical quest, a 'storming of the last earthly frontier' which could easily have 'developed into a new occult doctrine, a Kabbalah ...'

Less tormented, more conciliatory than *The Trial*, the novel mocks Kafka's heroic aspirations. Kafka's English translators, Edwin and Willa Muir, saw K. as Christian in *Pilgrim's Progress*, but perhaps *The Castle* transmutes all western myth: attacking patriarchy and stealing an older man's lover, K. recalls Oedipus. But he is agonized Hamlet, too, with whom he shares his own Rosencrantz and Guildenstern, the assistants Jeremias and Arthur. Then again, K. resembles Don Quixote – much evident in Kafka's writings now – as he tilts in futile battle with an imaginary foe. Somewhere beyond these phantoms lies the actual K., a mythic original: indecipherable modern man, defined relatively by role, absolutely by truth, and tragically caught by their clash, which even

Dora Dymant (1898–1952), Kafka's partner in 1923–4.

across an icy landscape ensnares the self in bureaucracy, annihilating human identity. K.'s modern, liberal demand for 'rights' cannot be met by a society still overshadowed by an authoritarian power. All this perhaps is symbolized by K.'s compromise: to live with his mistress among children in a schoolroom.

At the end of his life, Kafka himself achieved a brief idyll, when, having finally been pensioned off on 1 June 1922, he managed to escape Prague, and settled in Berlin for six months from September 1923 with the young Dora Dymant. They met just after his fortieth birthday at a Sabbath evening service for the children of the Berlin Jewish Holiday Home. She belonged to an orthodox eastern Jewish family. At first, they stayed in a room at 8 Miquelstrasse, then in two rooms at 13 Grunewaldstrasse, and finally at 25/26 Heidestrasse (now 7/9 Busseallee). The German economic crisis, with its notorious hyperinflation, exacted severe privations, and they had to depend on gifts of money and food parcels from Prague. In a memoir, Dora recalls some incidental and charming details, which capture the romance of their life: his dark skin, his long gait, his head to one side, his eyes open wide, his habit of talking 'with his fingers' rather than his hands, how they played Chinese shadows together, or how Kafka consoled a little girl who had lost her doll. He read her works like Hebel's *Unexpected Reunion* and E. T. A.

Hoffmann's *Tomcat Murr,* and Dora also describes the transformation he underwent when writing at

Grunewaldstrasse 13, in Berlin-Steglitz, where Kafka and Dora lived in 1923–4. Their landlady became the model for *A Little Woman.*

night. He had been working steadily for a while, at first on many texts produced in parallel to *The Castle*, notably *First Suffering* and *A Hunger Artist.* The latter is no pure invention, being based on a variety act which Kafka turns into a symbol for art as an existential performance, a prolonged act of dying

Kafka's parents in Bad Podiebrad (Poděbrady) in 1930.

enacted before an absent audience. He continued in Berlin with tales like *A Little Woman* (inspired by his landlady) and *The Burrow*, in which a solitary animal falls prey to its anxieties: Kafka told Dora that the animal's safe haven, Castle Square, symbolized her, but the ten paths leading from it also recall Prague's Old Town Square. A little later, back in Prague, his art attained a new, lucid ambiguity in his last work, *Josephine the Singer, or: The Mouse People*, which unites the contrary themes of politics and culture. In this, his final animal metamorphosis, Kafka meditates on both art and crowd behaviour among a fictive people that lives in thrall to a charismatic diva. In the end, artiste and community are ironically reconciled in death, when Josephine, 'the heroine of our people will be forgotten like all her brothers in transcendental redemption'.

His uncle, Doctor Siegfried Löwy, had visited him in Berlin, and, shocked at his condition, which had seriously deteriorated during the privations of the freezing winter, he pressed Kafka to return to Prague, after which Max Brod came to collect him. From Prague, in April 1924, Kafka travelled with Dora to a sanatorium in the Vienna Woods, where laryngeal tuberculosis was diagnosed. His case was hopeless, and he now had difficulty in speaking. Felix Weltsch visited him, and Werfel sent roses, together with his latest novel, *Verdi*. Then Kafka and Dora moved to a humble, ill-equipped sanatorium at Kierling, near Klosterneuburg. On 2 May the doctor diagnosed 'a degenerating tubercular process' in his larynx, which also affected his epiglottis. By now, the pain was unbearable, and Robert Klopstock came to nurse him. With Dora he formed what Kafka for the first time in his life regarded as his own 'little family'. It was too late. Max Brod paid a final call. A letter from Dora's father arrived, refusing her hand in marriage. Yet, despite his suffering, Kafka retained a capacity for pleasure, as when Robert Klopstock brought him the first cherries of the year. He particularly identified with the cut flowers in his room, admiring the lilac that 'drank' as it 'died'. Then, near the end, when an improvement was recorded, Kafka cried for joy at the prospect of recovery. By now, his treatment included two or three daily alcohol injections. With a superhuman effort, on 2 June, he wrote a long letter to his parents, which precisely narrates his circumstances, weighs up the pros and cons of a visit, and advises against it. Dora finished the letter, adding: 'I am taking the pen from his hand ... ' He suffered greatly that night, and asked Klopstock for morphine, saying: 'Kill me, or you're a murderer.' When Klopstock left to clean his syringe, Kafka pleaded: 'Don't leave me', and Klopstock said: 'I'm not going.' He replied: 'But I am' and closed his eyes. He died towards noon, a month before his forty-first birthday, and was buried in the Jewish Cemetery of Olsany (Friedhof von Olšany/Olšanské hřbitovy) at Straschnitz (Strašnice) in Prague.

Kafka's father, weakened by age, died in 1931, and his mother in 1934. Then, after Prague had been taken by the Nazis, in 1941 Elli and Valli were deported to Lodź, where, in 1942, they disappeared. In 1941, to avoid deportation, Uncle Siegfried Löwy took his own life. Ottla was taken to Theresienstadt (Terezín), and attended the inmates' sixtieth-birthday com-memoration of her brother. Later, she was transported to the east. She was killed in Auschwitz in 1943. Milena died in Ravensbrück. Felice and Dora survived, and Brod escaped to Palestine, taking Kafka's manuscripts with him.

The last photograph of Kafka (1923–4).

Dᴿ FRANZ KAFKA

1883–1924

יום ג' רח סיון תדפד' לב"ק
הל' הפקיר המפואר מור אנשיל שו'
בן הנעלה כר העניר לאאבמא_י
ונסם אבו יטל
ת נ צ ב ה

HERMANN KAFKA

1854–1931

ה'צ'ש נר יענ'קעה
בר המג בה 'עכב
ראפכא הכ בשק
סא _ן רבא לכן
אמו כ'ארלך

JULIE KAFKA

1856–1934

'אט'רה מ' יט' עהּ'ת
יעכבל'כר'תנוי רר
היע סאהּ_

Franz Kafka's grave, designed
by the Prague architect, Leopold
Ehrmenn. At the funeral, attended by family and friends , Max
Brod accompanied Dora. As the
coffin was lowered, she gave a
little scream and then mur-
mured the *Kaddish*, the Hebrew
prayer for the dead. Kafka's parents, Hermann and Julie, are
buried with their son.

References

Preface

p. 4 '*I have no literary interests...nothing else*': Kafka, *Briefe an Felice*, ed. Erich Heller and Jürgen Born, Frankfurt: Fischer, 1967, p. 444.

p. 5 '*alone as Franz Kafka*': Gustav Janouch, *Gespräche mit Kafka*, 2nd edn, Frankfurt: Fischer, 1968, p. 104.

p. 8 the '*negativity*' of the age: Kafka, *Hochzeitsvorbereitungen auf dem Lande*, ed. Max Brod, Frankfurt: Fischer, 1953, p. 120f.

p. 9 '*In the battle...the part of the world*': Kafka, *Nachgelassene Schriften und Fragmente II*, Kritische Ausgabe, ed. Jost Schillemeit, Frankfurt: Fischer, 1992, p. 58.

'*universal human weakness*': *Hochzeitsvorbereitungen*, p. 121.

'*I am an end or a beginninng*': *Hochzeitsvorbereitungen*, p. 121.

A Prague Childhood

p. 12 *'...in the middle...'*: Kafka, *Tagebücher*, Kritische Ausgabe, ed. Hans-Gerd Koch et al., Frankfurt: Fischer, 1990, p. 19.

p. 13 *'Kafka was Prague, and Prague was Kafka'*: Johannes Urzidil, *Da geht Kafka*, Stuttgart and Zurich: Artemis, 1963, p. 12.

p. 14 *'Prague...among the rubble'*: cited after H. G. Adler, 'Die Dichtung der Prager Schule' in *Im Brennpunkt ein Österreich*, ed. Manfred Wagner, Vienna: Europa Verlag, 1976, pp. 67–88; p. 79.

p. 18 *'What do I have in common...with myself'*: *Tagebücher*, p. 622.

Czech lay closer to his heart: Kafka, *Briefe an Milena*, revised edn, ed. Jürgen Born and Michael Müller, Frankfurt: Fischer, 1983, p. 17.

'Nothing can be achieved with a body like this' : *Tagebücher*, p. 263f.

'will for life, business, and conquest': Kafka, *Brief an den Vater*, in *Hochzeitsvorbereitungen*, pp. 162–223; see p. 164.

p. 25 *Kafka's earliest memories reflect this*: *Brief an den Vater*, p. 167.

p. 26 *Hugo Bergman*: Hugo Bergmann (sic), *Schulzeit und Studium* in: *'Als Kafka mir entgegenkam ...', Erinnerungen an Franz Kafka*, ed. Hans-Gerd Koch, Berlin: Wagenbach, 1995, pp. 13–24.

The Artist as Young Man

p. 28 *There is a coming and a going...*: Printed and reproduced in *Bergman*, p. 19f.

'one of whom went to America...': *Tagebücher*, p. 146.

p. 29 *'maybe for the tenth time'*: *Briefe an Felice*, p. 291.

the passage which he chose...: Klaus Wagenbach, *Franz Kafka: Eine Biographie seiner Jugend 1883–1912*, Bern: Francke, 1958, p. 63f.

p. 31 *'You could soar up to the...heavens'*: Hugo Bergman, *Tagebücher und Briefe I: 1901–1948*, ed. Miriam Sambursky, Königstein/Taunus: Athenäum Verlag, 1985, p. 9.

seven-point programme: *Nachgelassene Schriften und Fragmente II*, p. 105f.

p. 36 *'We burrow...velvet-furred'*: Kafka, *Briefe 1900–1912*, Kritische Ausgabe, ed. Hans-Gerd Koch, Frankfurt: Fischer, 1999, p. 40.

p. 38 *'The fruits...on the ground'*: Klaus Wagenbach, *Franz Kafka in Selbstzeugnissen und Bilddokumenten*, Reinbek bei Hamburg: Rowohlt, 1964, p. 42.

Prague café scene: Hartmut Binder, *Wo Kafka und seine Freunde zu Gast waren, Prager Kaffeehäuser und Vergnügungsstätten in historischen Bilddokumenten*, Prague: Vitalis, 2000, p. 222f.

p. 39 *'Have you already noticed...ploughed earth'*: *Briefe 1900–1912*, p. 16.

People who walk...: *Briefe 1900–1912*, p. 31.

p. 40 *'simultaneously understood as a nothing, a mere dream...'*: Kafka, *Beschreibung eines Kampfes*, Frankfurt: Fischer, 1946, p. 293.

'being in love with opposites': *Briefe 1900–1912*, p. 42.

I think we should only read...: *Briefe 1900–1912*, p. 36.

p. 44 *'I caused a bit of stir...'*: *Tagebucher*, p. 76.

I remember that first night...: Kafka, *Briefe an Milena*, p. 196f.

At the Workers' Accident Insurance

p. 46 *My life is now completely disorderly...*: *Briefe 1900–1912*, p. 72.

p. 48 *In Kafka's day...*: Kafka, *Amtliche Schriften*, ed.Klaus Hermsdrof, Berlin: Akademie Verlag, 1984, p. 9f.

p. 49 *'double life'*: *Tagebücher*, p. 29.

'Recently...we were head to head...': *Briefe an Felice*, p. 103.

he 'gives me strength...imitate': *Tagebücher*, p. 327.

pp. 49–50 *uncontrollable laughter in his presence*: *Briefe an Felice*, p. 238.

p. 50 *'On the extent of the obligation to insure in the building trade and in related trades'*: *Amtliche Schriften*, pp. 95–120.

p. 51 *When the interests of the workers...*: *Amtliche Schriften*, p. 120.

pp. 52–3 *'Who has a magic hand...a thousand knives'*: *Tagebücher*, p. 596f.

pp. 53–4 *'How modest...with requests...'*: Max Brod, *Franz Kafka: Eine Biographie*, 3rd edn, Frankfurt: Fischer, 1954, p. 102.

p. 54 *Yesterday in the factory...*: *Tagebücher*, p. 373f.

'...these two professions can never tolerate one another': *Tagebücher*, pp. 32–5.

'A single shot...': Max Brod/Franz Kafka: *Eine Freundschaft II, Briefwechsel*, ed. Malcolm Pasley, Frankfurt: Fischer, 1989, p. 74.

The Making of a Writer

p. 58 *'enormous member'*: *Tagebücher*, p. 275.

blind child...cheekbone: *Tagebücher*, p. 49f.

sliced up like a sausage: *Tagebücher*, p. 560.

'This morning for the first time...': *Tagebücher*, p. 220.

'The representation of my dream-like inner world...': *Tagebücher*, p. 546.

'the terrible uncertainty of my inner existence': *Tagebücher*, p. 559.

p. 60 *'blood relative'*: *Briefe an Felice*, p. 460.

'almost completely under Max's influence': *Tagebücher*, p. 198.

'Max does not understand me...': *Briefe an Felice*, p. 559.

p. 61 *'wonderful places'*: *Briefe an Felice*, p. 178.

'Because I didn't have anything for a tip...': *Briefe 1900–1912*, p. 80

...in the empty office...: *Briefe 1900–1912*, p. 82.

p. 62 *'Trocadero. He's in love...'*: Max Brod, *Über Franz Kafka*, Frankfurt: Fischer, 1974, p. 104.

'had been ridden over by entire cavalry regiments': Brod, *Über Franz Kafka*, p. 104.

The three little doors...: *Tagebücher*, p. 48.

p. 63 *'Stiff hips..."Spring Mood"'*: *Tagebücher*, p. 44.

pp. 63–4 *'A witty tragedian...changing lights...'*: *Tagebücher*, p. 148.

p. 66 *'Perhaps I will one day manage to say...'*: Kafka, *Briefe 1902–1924*, ed. Max Brod, Frankfurt: Fischer, 1958, p. 130.

'utter rubbish': Hanns Zischler, *Kafka geht ins Kino*, Reinbek bei Hamburg: Rowohlt, 1996, p. 47.

'cinematographic': *Tagebücher*, p. 564.

'I was a great draughtsman...anything else': *Briefe an Felice*, p. 294.

p. 68 *'junk room'*: *Tagebücher*, p. 266.

The Breakthrough

p. 69 *'We had never seen an aeroplane...'*: Brod, *Über Franz Kafka*, p. 92.

wings 'shining in the sun': Kafka, 'Die Aeroplane in Brescia', in *Drucke zu Lebzeiten*, Kritische Ausgabe, ed. Wolff Kittler et al., Frankfurt: Fischer, 1994, p. 409.

p. 70 *'free-word' style*: see Max Brod/Franz Kafka: *Eine Freund-schaft, I, Reiseaufzeichnungen*, ed. Malcolm Pasley, Frankfurt:

Fischer, 1987, p. 37f.

p. 71 *Moi je flâne...*: *Reiseaufzeichnungen*, p. 50.

in a Futurist way: see *Reiseaufzeichnungen*, p. 182.

describes a car crash: *Reiseaufzeichnungen*, pp. 185–8.

p. 74 *'lethargic Judaism'*: *Tagebücher*, p. 349.

'the Bible of the Kabbalists': *Tagebücher*, p. 366.

p. 75 *'noble culture of German letters'*: cited after Roger Hermes et al., *Franz Kafka: Eine Chronik*, Berlin: Wagenbach, 1999, p. 40.

view Halley's Comet: *Tagebücher*, p. 16.

p. 76 *'by chance'*: *Briefe an Felice*, p. 218. On the publication history of *Meditation*, see *Drucke zu Lebzeiten*, pp. 35–44.

'poor work': *Eine Freundschaft, II Briefwechsel*, p. 110.

For we are like tree-trunks...: *Drucke zu Lebzeiten*, p. 33.

p. 78 *I wrote this story...*: *Tagebücher*, p. 660f.

p. 79 *'a walk around' his family*: *Briefe an Felice*, pp. 394 and 435.

p. 80 *'cannot be explained'*: *Briefe an Felice*, p. 394.

p. 81 *'which came to me...in bed'*: *Briefe an Felice*, p. 102.

'I'm so sorry about this...': *Briefe an Felice*, p. 125.

p. 82 *natural 'drive'*: *Briefe an Felice*, p. 125.

'Cry, my beloved...a little while ago': *Briefe an Felice*, p. 160.

'Dearest...no doubt about it': *Briefe an Felice*, p. 163.

'a spineless creature': *Drucke zu Lebzeiten*, p. 118.

The Great War

p. 85 *'salvation'*: *Briefe an Felice*, p. 368.

'somehow communicate...my heart': *Briefe an Felice*, p. 368.

p. 86 *'unshakeable judgement'*: *Tagebücher*, pp. 431f.

'I cannot live...without her': *Briefe an Felice*, p. 380f.

p. 87 *'I cannot believe...perhaps forever'*: *Briefe an Felice*, p. 730.

'bound like a criminal...could not have been worse': *Tagebücher*, p. 528.

The trip in the cab...: *Tagebücher*, p. 658f.

p. 90 *...a series of terrible days...*: Brod/Kafka, *Briefwechsel*, p. 147.

p. 91 *'If I don't rescue myself...'*: *Tagebücher*, p. 542f.

p. 92 *'Begun failed works...'*: *Tagebücher*, p. 543.

pp. 92–3 *'I have no time...more decided than ever'*: *Tagebücher*, p. 543.

p. 93 *'Germany...swimming school'*: *Tagebücher*, p. 545.

'I am shattered...31 years old...': *Tagebücher*, p. 545.

pp. 93–4 *Just as he had originally conceived* The Judgement...: *Briefe an Felice*, p. 394.

p. 94 *'End of writing...'*: *Tagebücher*, p. 721.

'blood relatives': *Briefe an Felice*, p. 460.

pp. 95–6 *'The Court...when you go'*: Kafka, *Der Process*, Kritische Ausgabe, ed.Malcolm Pasley, Frankfurt: Fischer, 1990, p. 304.

p. 97 'the world order': *Der Process*, p. 303.

p. 98 *sexual inadequacies*: *Briefe an Felice*, p. 271.

What fascinates him about Napoleon's 'error'...: *Tagebücher*, pp. 757–64.

p. 99 '*The next task...soldier*': *Briefe an Felice*, p. 511.

'*candidates for the lunatic asylum*': *Briefe an Felice*, p. 764.

The Final Rupture

p. 102 '*down the castle steps to the old town*': *Briefe an Felice*, p. 750.

'*enormous wound*': *Ein Landarzt, Drucke zu Lebzeiten*, p. 258.

p. 104 *You have the chance...*: Kafka, *Tagebücher*, p. 831

p. 105 '*to elevate life...*': *Tagebücher*, p. 838.

'*small, good marriage*': *Briefe 1902–1924*, p. 164.

p. 107 '*I err. The true way...*': *Nachgelassene Schriften und Fragmente II*, p. 30.

'*To grasp the good fortune...*': *Nachgelassene Schriften und Fragmente II*, p. 118.

pp. 107–8 '*Believing means...being*': *Nachgelassene Schriften und Fragmente II*, p. 55.

p. 108 '*The crows maintain...*': *Nachgelassene Schriften und Fragmente II*, p. 51.

It is not actually the material world...senses': *Nachgelassene Schriften und Fragmente II*, p. 124.

p. 109 *It was very early in the morning...*: *Nachgelassene Schriften und Fragmente II*, p. 530.

p. 110 *I now spend every afternoon...*: *Briefe an Milena*, p. 288.

The Last Earthly Frontier

p. 111 *'servant of a God...believe'*: Franz Blei, 'Franz Kafka' in *Schriften in Auswahl*, ed. A. P. Gütersloh, Munich: Biederstein, 1960, p. 295.

p. 112 *'smashed and elevated'*: *Tagebücher*, p. 433.

p. 114 *'western Jew'*: *Tagebücher*, p. 563.

p. 116 *simple 'spirituality'*: Ernst Weiss, 'Mozart: Ein Meister des Ostens' in *Das Unverlierbare*, Berlin: Rowohlt, 1928, pp. 9–34.

'at the moment when it cracks': Brod, *Über Franz Kafka*, p. 70.

'For some time I have been complaining of an illness...': *Tagebücher*, pp. 49–52.

p. 117 *'From a certain point, there is no going back...'*: *Nachgelassene Schriften und Fragmente II*, p. 34.

p. 119 *'a living fire such as I have never seen before'*: *Briefe 1902–1924*, p. 275.

'My world is collapsing...': *Briefe an Milena*, p. 57.

'too weak to join him': Brod, *Franz Kafka*, p. 286f.

p. 122 *We all seem to be able...*: Brod, *Franz Kafka*, p. 281f.

p. 124 *'I only relate to the medical student...'*: *Briefe 1902–1924*, p. 323.

'Tuberculosis...only one disease...': *Briefe 1902–1924*, p. 320.

'I can't even bear people's gaze...': *Briefe 1902–1924*, p. 357.

nervous 'collapse': *Tagebücher*, p. 877.

'nocturnal decision': *Tagebücher*, p. 885.

'If there is a transmigration of souls...': *Tagebücher*, p. 888.

'Joseph K.': *Tagebücher*, p. 893.

p. 126 *'The strange...comfort of writing...'*: *Tagebücher*, p. 892.

Assaults on the path...: *Tagebücher*, p. 894.

p. 127 *The clearest thing...*: *Tagebücher*, p. 903f.

a 'storming of the last earthly frontier...Kabbalah...': *Tagebücher*, p. 878.

p. 128 *In a memoir*: Dora Dymant, 'Mein Leben mit Franz Kafka' in *Als Kafka mir entgegenkam*, pp. 174–85.

p. 131 *'the heroine...redemption'*: *Drucke zu Lebzeiten*, p. 377.

a...sanatorium...near Klosterneuberg: Rotraut Hackemüller, *Kafkas letzte Jahre 1917–1924*, Munich: Kirchheim, 1990, p. 126f.

p. 132 *'drank' as it 'died'*: *Briefe 1902–1924*, pp. 489 and 491.

'I am taking the pen from his hand...': Kafka, *Briefe an die Eltern aus den Jahren 1922–1924*, ed. Josef Čermak and Martin Svatoš, Prague: Odeon, 1990, p. 150f.

p. 132 *'Kill me, or you're a murderer'*: Brod, *Über Franz Kafka*, p. 189.

Chronology

1883	Born 3 July near Old Town Square, Prague.
1889–93	Attends primary school, on the Meat Market (am Fleischmarkt/Masný trh).
	Friendship with Hugo Bergman.
1893–1901	Attends the German Gymnasium, Kinský Palais, Old Town Square.
	Friendship with Oskar Pollak.
1896	Celebrates his *bar mitzvah* on 13 June.
1901–6	Studies at the German Charles Ferdinand University, Prague.
1901–5	Joins Reading and Lecture Hall of the German Students in Prague.
1902	Friendship with Max Brod.
	Forms literary circle with Max Brod, Felix Weltsch, and Oskar Baum. Meets members of the Louvre Circle around Franz Brentano, and the Fanta Salon.
1904	Begins *Description of a Struggle*.

1906–7	Practical work as a lawyer.
1907–8	Works at *Assicurazioni Generali*, at 19 Wenceslas Square (Wenzelsplatz/Václavské náměstí).
1907	Begins *Wedding Preparations in the Country*.
1908–22	Works at Workers' Accident Insurance Company, at 7 Na Poříčí.
1908	Friendship with Willy Haas and Franz Werfel. Franz Blei visits Prague. Publishes eight texts, entitled *Meditation*, in Blei's periodical, *Hyperion*.
1909	Begins extant *Diaries*. Holiday in Riva with Max and Otto Brod. Publishes *The Aeroplanes in Brescia*.
1910	First trip to Paris. Attends readings and lectures by Karl Kraus, Adolf Loos, Rudolf Steiner and Albert Einstein.
1911	Meets Alfred Kubin. Second Paris trip. Meets the actor Jizchak Löwy, and other members of the Yiddish Theatre Troupe. With Brod starts travel novel, *Richard and Samuel* (unfinished). Writings include *A Loud Noise* and *The Fate of the Bachelor*.
1912	Begins *The Lost One*. Attends a performance by Frank Wedekind and a reading by Hugo von Hofmannsthal. Holds lecture on Yiddish language to introduce a reading by Jizchak Löwy, Jewish Town Hall. In the summer meets Ernst Rowohlt and Kurt Wolff. Visits Goethe House in Weimar. In Prague: meets Felice Bauer. In the autumn writes *The Judgement* and *The Metamorphosis*. Rowohlt publishes *Meditation*. In December gives public reading of *The Judgement*, at the Hotel Archduke Ferdinand (now Hotel Europa), Wenceslas Square.

1913	Meets Martin Buber. Friendship with Ernst Weiss. Part-time work as a gardener. Publication of *The Judgement* in *Arcadia*, and *The Stoker* by Kurt Wolff. Holidays in Vienna, Venice, and Riva. Meets the 'Swiss girl'. Recites from Kleist's *Michael Kohlhaas*, Toynbee Hall, Jewish Town Hall.
1914	Engaged to Felice Bauer on 1 June. The engagement annulled on 12 July. Writes *The Trial* (to January 1915), *Memories of the Kalda Railway*, *In the Penal Colony*, *The Village Schoolmaster* (= *The Giant Mole*).
1915	Renewed meeting with Felice. Carl Sternheim donates Kafka the Fontane Prize. Writes *Blumfeld, an Elderly Bachelor*. Publishes *The Metamorphosis* in *Die weissen Blätter* and as a book with Kurt Wolff.
1916	Meets Martin Buber and Robert Musil. With Felice in Marienbad. Recites *In the Penal Colony* at Galerie Goltz, Munich. Ottla rents house for him in Golden Lane. Writes *The Hunter Gracchus* and *A Report for an Academy*. Kurt Wolff publishes *The Judgement*, and second edition of *The Stoker*.
1917	Writes *The Bucket Rider, The Great Wall of China, Eleven Sons, On the Gallery, A Hybrid*. Burns several manuscripts. Rents rooms in Schönborn Palais. Writes *A Country Doctor*. Starts to learn Hebrew. In July: visits Hungary with Felice. Second engagement. Coughs blood in the night of 12–13 August. Tuberculosis is diagnosed. Moves to his sister Ottla at Zürau (Siřem) (until Spring 1918). From October writes aphorisms in *Reflections on Sin, Suffering,*

Hope, and the True Way (to February 1918), and other short texts, including *An Everyday Occurrence*, *The Truth about Sancho Panza*, *The Silence of the Sirens*. In December annuls second engagement to Felice.

1918   Returns to Prague. Goes to Schelesen (Želízy) in the autumn. Meets Julie Wohryzek.

1919   Summer in Prague. Engagement to Julie. Autumn in Schelesen. Writes *Letter to my Father*. Kurt Wolff publishes *In the Penal Colony* and the collection *A Country Doctor*.

1920   Writes aphorisms in *He*. To Merano. Correspondence with Milena Jesenská. Breaks with Julie. Visits Milena in Vienna. Goes to sanatorium in Vienna Woods. Summer and autumn in Prague. Meets Milena in Gmünd. Writes many short texts, including *A City Coat-of-Arms*, *Poseidon*, *The Problem of Our Laws*, *The Vulture*, *Little Fable*. In December goes to a sanatorium in Matliary in the High Tatras. Friendship with Robert Klopstock.

1921   Matliary. Returns to Prague in August. Makes last will. Gives *Diaries* to Milena. Ludwig Hardt recites *A Country Doctor* and other tales in the Mozarteum, Prague, and *Eleven Sons* and other works in the Secession, Berlin.

1922   To Spindelmühle (Špindlerův Mlýn) in the Giant Mountains. Begins *The Castle* (January to August). Goes to Prague late February. Writes *First Suffering*, *A Hunger Artist*. On 1 July retires on health grounds. With Ottla in Planá from late June to September. Writes *Investigations of a Dog*, *The Married Couple*, *A Comment* (= *Give it up!*).

1923	In Berlin with Dora Dymant from September. Writes *A Little Woman*, *The Burrow* (to 1924).
1924	Ludwig Hardt recites *A Report for an Academy* in the Meistersaal, Berlin. Dora attends. Returns to Prague with Dora and Brod in March. Writes *Josephine the Singer*. His voice fails. Suffers great pain. Visits various clinics in Austria. In April goes to a sanatorium at Kierling, near Klosterneuburg. Has difficulty reading. In May proof-reads the collection *A Hunger Artist* (published in August by Die Schmiede). Dies towards noon on 3 June. Buried in Prague-Strašnice 11 June.

Bibliography

Kafka's novels

America, translated by Edwin Muir with a Postscript by Max
    Brod (London: Secker & Warburg (1938), definitive edn
    1949). The standard version based on Brod's text.
The Man who Disappeared (Amerika), translated by Michael
    Hoffmann (London: Penguin, 1996). A new version based
    on the critical edition.
The Trial. With Unfinished Chapters, translated by Willa and
    Edwin Muir (London: Secker & Warburg (1935), definitive
    edn 1956). The standard version based on Brod's text,
    revised with additional chapters and notes by E. M. Butler.
    Includes the fragmentary chapters.
The Trial, translated by Idris Parry (London: Penguin, 1994).
    A new version based on the critical edition.
The Castle, translated by Willa and Edwin Muir (London:
    Secker & Warburg, 1957). The standard version based on

Brod's text, with additional notes and material by Eithne Wilkins and Ernst Kaiser.

The Castle, translated by J. A. Underwood, with an Introduction by Idris Parry (London: Penguin, 1997). A new version based on the critical edition.

The Castle. A New Translation based on the Restored Text, translated by Mark Harman (New York: Schocken Books, 1999). A new version that closely follows the critical edition.

The Complete Novels, translated by Willa and Edwin Muir (*The Castle*, 1930; *The Trial*, 1935; *Amerika*, 1938) (London: Vintage Classics, 1999). Compendium edition of the versions which established Kafka's international reputation. They are also available individually.

Kafka's stories

Metamorphosis and other Stories, translated by Edwin and Willa Muir (London: Secker & Warburg, 1949; London: Vintage Classics, 1999). Contains six stories.

Wedding Preparations in the Country, translated by Ernst Kaiser and Eithne Wilkins (London: Secker & Warburg/ New York: Schocken (as *Dearest Father: Stories and Other Writings*), 1954). Includes *Letter to my Father* and the aphorisms.

Description of a Struggle and The Great Wall of China, translated by Willa and Edwin Muir (London: Secker & Warburg, 1960). A generous selection.

Metamorphosis and other Stories, translated and edited by Malcolm Pasley (London: Penguin, 2000 (originally published under the title *Transformation and other Stories*)). An authoritative text.

The Great Wall of China and Other Shorter Works, translated and edited by Malcolm Pasley (London: Penguin, 1973).

An authoritative text. Includes the aphorisms.

The Complete Short Stories, edited by Nahum H. Glatzer, with a Foreword by John Updike (New York: Schocken, 1983). A good commentated edition.

Stories 1904–1924, translated by J. A. Underwood, with a Foreword by Jorge Luis Borges (London: Abacus, 2000). All collections published by Kafka himself.

Letters, Diaries, Conversations

Letters to Friends, Family, and Editors, edited by Max Brod, translated by Richard and Clara Winston (London: Secker & Warburg/New York: Schocken, 1977).

Letters to Felice, edited by Erich Heller and Jürgen Born, translated by James Stern and Elisabeth Duckworth (London: Secker & Warburg/New York: Schocken, 1974; London: Vintage Classics, 1999).

Letters to Milena, edited by Willy Haas, translated by Tania and James Stern (London: Secker & Warburg/New York: Schocken, 1953; London: Vintage Classics, 1999).

The Diaries of Franz Kafka, edited by Max Brod: Vol. 1 (1910–1923) translated by Joseph Kresch (London: Secker & Warburg, 1948); Vol. 2 (1914–1923) translated by Martin Greenberg with the cooperation of Hannah Arendt (London: Secker & Warburg, 1948) (Reprinted in one volume, London: Vintage Classics, 1999).

Gustav Janouch, *Conversations with Kafka: Notes and Reminiscences*, with an Introduction by Max Brod, translated by Goronwy Rees (London: Derek Verschoyle, 1953; revised 2nd edn, London: Andre Deutsch, 1968).

Biographies

Johann Bauer and Isidor Pollak, *Kafka and Prague*, translated by P. S. Falla (London: Pall Mall, 1971).

Max Brod, *Franz Kafka: A Biography*, translated by G. H. Roberts (London: Secker & Warburg, 1947; 2nd edn 1960, New York: Da Capo Press, 1995).

Pietro Citati, *Kafka*, translated from the Italian by Raymond Rosenthal (London: Secker & Warburg, 1990).

Pavel Eisner, *Franz Kafka and Prague* (New York: Arts Inc., 1950).

Jiří Gruša, *Franz Kafka of Prague*, translated by Erich Mosbacher (London: Secker & Warburg, 1985)

Ronald Hayman, *A Biography of Franz Kafka* (London: Weidenfeld & Nicholson, 1981).

Peter Mailloux, *A Hesitation before Birth: The Life of Franz Kafka* (Newark, London, and Toronto: University of Delaware Press, 1989).

Anthony Northey, *Kafka's Relatives: Their Lives and his Writing* (New Haven and London: Yale University Press, 1991)

Ernst Pawel, *The Nightmare of Reason: A Life of Franz Kafka* (London: Harvill, 1984).

Klaus Wagenbach, *Franz Kafka: Pictures of a Life*, translated by Arthur S. Wensinger (New York: Pantheon Books, 1984).

The Historico-Cultural Context

Peter Demetz, *Prague in Black and Gold: The History of a City* (London, Allen Lane, 1997).

John Hibberd, *Kafka in Context* (London: Studio Vista, 1975).

Jan Kaplan and Krystynne Nosarzewzka, *Prague: The Turbulent Century. A Visual History of the Twentieth Century* (Cologne: Könemann, 1997).

Angelo Maria Ripellino, *Magic Prague*, translated by David Newton Marinelli (London: Macmillan, 1994; London: Picador, 1995).

Derek Sayer, *The Coasts of Bohemia: A Czech History* (New Jersey: Princeton University Press, 1998).

Scott Spector, *Prague Territories: National Conflict and Cultural Innovation in Franz Kafka's Fin de Siècle* (Berkeley, Los Angeles and London: University of California Press, 2000).

J. P. Stern (ed.), *The World of Franz Kafka* (London: Weidenfeld, 1980).

Critical Studies

Robert Alter, *Necessary Angels: Tradition and Modernity in Kafka, Benjamin, and Scholem* (Cambridge Mass.: Harvard University Press, 1991).

Mark Anderson, *Kafka's Clothes: Ornament and Aestheticism in the Habsburg fin de siecle* (Oxford, Clarendon Press, 1992).

Harold Bloom (ed.), *Franz Kafka: Modern Critical Essays* (New York: Chelsea House, 1986).

Elias Canetti, *Kafka's Other Trial: The Letters to Felice,* translated by Christopher Middleton (London: Calder & Boyars/ New York: Schocken, 1974).

Angel Flores (ed.), *The Kafka Problem* (New York: New Directions, 1946).

Angel Flores (ed.), *The Kafka Debate: New Perspectives for our Time* (New York: Gordian Press, 1977)

Ronald Gray (ed.), *Kafka: A Collection of Critical Essays,* Twentieth Century Views (Eaglewood Cliffs, NJ: Prentice Hall, 1962).

Erich Heller, *Kafka*, Modern Masters Series (London: Fontana, 1974).

Charles Osborne, *Franz Kafka*, Writers and Critics Series (Edinburgh and London: Olivers & Boyd, 1967).

Heinz Politzer, *Franz Kafka: Parable and Paradox* (Ithaca, NY: Cornell University Press, 1962; revised edn, 1966).

Ritchie Robertson, *Kafka: Judaism, Politics, and Literature* (Oxford: Clarendon Press, 1985).

Walter Sokel, *Franz Kafka*, Columbia Essays on Modern Writers (New York and London: Columbia University Press, 1966).

Meno Spann, *Franz Kafka*, Twayne's World Author Series (Boston: Twayne, 1976).

J. P. Stern and J. J.White (eds.), *Paths and Labyrinths: Nine Papers from a Kafka Symposium* (London: Publications of the Institute of Germanic Studies 35, 1985).

Anthony Thorlby, *A Student's Guide to Kafka* (London: Heine-mann, 1972).

Johannes Urzidil, *There goes Kafka*, translated by Harold A. Basilius (Detroit: Wayne State University Press, 1968).

List of Illustrations
and Photographic Acknowledgements

Every effort has been made to contact all copyright holders. The publishers will be happy to make good in future editions any errors or omissions brought to their attention.

Page

ii Kafka in a bowler hat. (Archiv Klaus Wagenbach, Berlin)
4 K. Bellmann, *Prague from Letná Hill.* (Jan Kaplan)
5 Prague Castle. (Jan Kaplan)
6–7 Prague skyline from the road beneath Chotek Park. (Jan Kaplan)
8 Old Town Square with Town Hall. (Jan Kaplan)
10 Kafka aged 5. (Archiv Klaus Wagenbach, Berlin)
11 Kafka's birthplace. (Jan Kaplan)
12 Clearance of Prague Ghetto. (Jan Kaplan)
13 Niklasstrasse. (Jan Kaplan)
14 Kafka's father. (Archiv Klaus Wagenbach, Berlin)
15 Kafka's mother. (Archiv Klaus Wagenbach, Berlin)

92 (*bottom*) Soldiers in Prague during the First World War. (Jan Kaplan)

93 Karel Šviha. (Private Collection)

95 František Drtikol *The Courtyards of Prague, No. 11*, 1911. (Museum of Decorative Arts, Prague)

96 Josef Sudek, photograph of St Vitus's Cathedral, from a series, 1924–28. (© 1990 Estate of Josef Sudek, *Josef Sudek: Poet of Prague: A Photographer's Life* © 1990 Aperture Foundation, Inc. Photo: Museum of Decorative Arts, Prague)

98 Adolphe Roehn, *Bivouac de Napoléon sur le champ de bataille de Wagram, nuit de 5–6 juillet, 1809*, (Musée du Château, Versailles. Photo: AKG London/VISIOARS)

100 The house at Bilekgasse. (Archiv Klaus Wagenbach, Berlin)

101 (*top*) Jindřich Tomec, *Nerudova*, 1907. From *Královské Hlani Město Praha* (Prague: Praha Vydano, 1911)

101 (*bottom*) Drawing from Kafka's octavo notebook. (Archiv Klaus Wagenbach, Berlin)

102 (*top*) The house at 22 Golden Lane. (Jan Kaplan)

102 (*bottom*) The old steps, the Prague castle. (Archiv Klaus Wagenbach, Berlin)

104 Siegfried Löwy having his motorcycle pushed. (Archiv Klaus Wagenbach, Berlin)

105 (*left*) Elli aged 21. (Archiv Klaus Wagenbach, Berlin)

105 (*right*) Valli aged 20. (Archiv Klaus Wagenbach, Berlin)

106 Kafka with Ottla at the entrance to their home in Zürau. (Archiv Klaus Wagenbach, Berlin)

108 View of Zürau. (Archiv Klaus Wagenbach, Berlin)

112 Kafka's proof corrections to the title page of *A Country Doctor*. From H. Siebenschein et al., *Franz Kafka a Praha* (Prague: Vladimir Žikeš, 1947)

113 Cover of first edition of *In the Penal Colony*, 1919. (Archiv Klaus Wagenbach, Berlin)

114 Kafka and Ernst Weiss, holidaying at Marielyst. (Archiv Klaus Wagenbach, Berlin)